# The Parent-Child Connection

# The
# Parent-Child
# Connection

Wm. Lee Carter

**BAKER BOOK HOUSE**
Grand Rapids, Michigan 49516

Copyright 1989 by
Baker Book House Company

Printed in the United States of America

**Library of Congress Cataloging-in-Publication Data**

Carter, William Lee, 1925–
    The parent-child connection / William Lee Carter.
        p.   cm.
    ISBN 0-8010-2542-7
    1. Parent and child. 2. Child rearing. 3. Communication in the
family.   I. Title.
HQ755.85.C363   1989
306.874—dc20                                                    89-39602
                                                                      CIP

Bible translations used are the Revised Standard Version (RSV), the New
International Version (NIV), the King James Version (KJV) and the Good News
Bible (GNB).

Cover and interior photos by Jim Whitmer.

# Contents

## Part 3: Effective Communication

# Preface

Wouldn't it be marvelous if children came into the world with enclosed instructions telling how to properly raise them? I've heard many veteran parents declare that if they were allowed to start over in raising their family, many things would be done differently. Unfortunately, most parents raise children by trial and error.

I have yet to hear parents say they don't care about their children's well-being. No parents enter their roles as caretakers intending to foul things up.

However, children are quite complex. Just when we feel we are on the right track with them, a seemingly unsolvable problem arises. As parents, we wonder what elements we have failed to provide in the home. We no longer know what to say to our children. Discipline appears to be totally ineffective.

The purpose of this book is to examine the connection between the parent and child. Issues dealt with in the following pages will help define the parent's role in shaping the behavior of the child. I am writing from the point of view that there are three primary areas of responsibility in the role of the parent.

The parent has the initial responsibility of providing a home environment that takes into account the psychological needs of the child. Although all family members are viewed as having equal value, it is the parent who must assume the position of leadership in the home. To allow a child to control the atmosphere of the home is harmful to that child's development.

Second, the parent must have a well-organized system of managing the behavior of the child. To resort to random methods of punishing and rewarding the child is confusing at best. The parent who has a systematic plan of action can deal more effectively and efficiently with problem behaviors.

Third, I see effective communication with children as being the best tool parents can use to help children reach their potential. I have never talked with children or adolescents who did not want to be understood by their parents. Yet, proficiency in communication is among the most difficult of social skills to develop.

I have chosen to depict common situations found in families to illustrate the concepts presented in the text of this book. As you read, you may find that you have shared similar frustrations and successes to those of the families in the illustrations. The ideas are applicable to all ages of childhood and adolescence.

The role of the parent is not an easy one. Our children are capable of involving us in the most perplexing dilemmas we will face during our lifetime. It is my hope that in the following pages you will find useful guidance and direction as you strive toward wholeness in your designated relationship with your child.

PART **1**

# Establishing the Home Atmosphere

*For this child I prayed; and the LORD*
*has granted me my petition*
(1 SAM. 1:27 RSV).

# 1

# The Right Atmosphere Is Vital

You've met the Johnsons before. You've probably been in their home; in fact, you may live there! Theirs is the household in which the television is always on with the volume high, and at least two radios are playing—different stations, of course. The children, who are not watching the television nor listening to either radio, are playing a game that is a modified version of World War II. Mother is screaming at the kids in an effort to move them toward the bathtub. Dad has conveniently slipped outside to feed the family dog, who has chased the neighbor's cat up a tree. What an atmosphere!

As a psychologist, the first goal I strive to attain is to have people feel comfortable when they talk with me. They must feel safe so that psychological growth can take place. Unless the atmosphere allows psychological growth, any effort to provide a client a rewarding experience will be fruitless. A successful parent, who in many ways is the child's own personal therapist, cannot do an adequate job rearing a child in an atmosphere such as the one in the Johnson's house. Let's take a moment to examine it.

The mood in the Johnson's household is one of chaos. There is no purpose in the behavior of the individual family members except to avoid meaningful contact with one another. No one is listening to anyone else, but is busy "doing his own thing," concerned only with the moment and not about the other family members. Certainly, the level of communication among the Johnsons is quite low, and there is little sense of warmth. Worst of all, the same scene of madness is doomed to repeat itself over and over again.

Countless parents have been bewildered by the evasive art of childrearing. Those who have become successful parents have discovered that there is more to childrearing than simply applying basic behavior management techniques or communicating openly with children. While these areas are of utmost importance (and will be discussed in sections 2 and 3), the first ingredient in successfully dealing with children at home is an atmosphere in which growth can take place. In the chapters of this section, the various elements of a proper home atmosphere will be identified and discussed.

Although many of the ideas in the next few chapters may seem elementary, my experience with and observation of a wide range of families from different social and economic levels suggests that these elements are often missing in their homes. I will be writing from the point of view that it is the parents, not the child, who bear the responsibility for establishing the atmosphere of the home.

While the parents are the leaders in the home and are responsible for setting the atmosphere, it is important for them to believe that no family member has more worth or value than any other. For ages there has been something of an unwritten standard that within the family structure it is the older family members who dominate, even rule, the younger family members. The child is the "low man on the totem pole" and is to "be seen and not heard." Parents are dictators and policy makers rather than equals.

However, it is a fundamental spiritual concept that a human's worth does not change from infancy through the end of adulthood. The life of a newborn child is viewed by God as being of equal value to the life of an elderly adult. By equals, I am not advocating that children be allowed to take their turn in governing the house. I am suggesting that children have an equal claim with the parents to be respected and to share responsibility in the home. In the same way that Mother and Dad want to be assured of their worth to others, so, too, the child is entitled to that assurance.

As parents we would do well to move away from the concept that the parent is the child's superior. In the ideal family structure, no one is superior to anyone else. Each family member simply has a different role to fulfill. It is because of the parents' age, experience in life, and knowledge of worldly and spiritual matters that they are the leaders of the family, not because they have more worth than the children. The first task, then, of the parent—the leader—is to set the atmosphere in the home so children can grow to have a healthy sense of responsibility and feeling of worth.

*He must manage his own children*
*well and see that his children obey*
*him with proper respect*
(1 TIM. 3:4-5 NIV).

# 2

# What Do You Think?

All parents have a system of beliefs about the general nature of children, whether or not they realize it. Some parents believe that children are naturally prone toward negative behavior. Most American religions teach that we are all born with a tendency to sin. It is true that we all commit sinful deeds daily. Yet, some parents take this belief and assume that it is their responsibility to "harness the lion" in their children, which may foster the idea that children are basically untrustworthy and must be very closely guarded if they are to keep from developing bad traits.

Mrs. Washington followed Kelly practically everywhere she went. She felt the need to check on most things her daughter did. Her commands and suggestions were frequent: "You don't need to go swimming today," or "That book is too hard for you to read," or "Don't forget to wash behind your ears," or "I'd better not get a telephone call from your teacher today." She made an effort to know as much about her daughter's friends as possible, for she did not want her child to run around with the wrong crowd! Each day after school she checked with Kelly to see if she had homework to complete. On the days Kelly said she had no homework, Mrs. Washington might call the parents of some of Kelly's classmates to be sure the girl was being truthful.

It sounds as though Mrs. Washington had a low level of faith in Kelly. Indeed she did! Her belief system held that children are prone toward the development of negative behaviors and should not have the autonomy to make decisions on their own. Children must be provided an abundance of direction if they are ever going to amount to anything positive, and it is a good thing they have parents to save them from the path of evil!

We all realize that every child will be naughty or contrary from time to time. Admittedly, many children seem to portray a negative image most of the time! Despite this tendency, however, all children have an inborn motivation to develop positive characteristics. That is, there is something within each child that gives him or her value; every child has the potential to become good. We can be assured of each child's goodness because of the God-given worth of each human life.

Every adult knows at least one child, probably more, whom even the most generous observer would not rate as being "good." What is it, then, that separates the good apples from the bad, the well-rounded child from the one who is disturbed and hard to like? The answer to this question may be at least partially found by inspecting the child's various basic needs—needs that must be adequately met in establishing a healthy home atmosphere.

We all know that every child has primary needs for such things as food, clothing, comfortable living conditions, and companionship. Most people would also agree that the need for love is one that is shared by all children, the need to be valued with no strings or conditions attached. But we tend to underestimate its importance.

A youngster whose need for love is not satisfied will develop a distrust of others, will be fearful, will often question the sincerity of those who demonstrate faith in the child or act kindly.

An eight-year-old boy, Terry, visited a counselor for the first time. He came from a home that offered him little in the way of emotional support. His parents showed sparse amounts of love toward one another and certainly did not display tender emotions toward him. He was generally known as an aggressive boy who did not get along with many people and who was not well-liked by other children. Terry was uncertain how to act when the counselor ushered him into his office.

Through the course of their time together, Terry was rather uncomfortable. He had difficulty choosing appropriate responses to this man. But Terry was impressed by the fact that the counselor didn't seem to judge his every move with criticism and apparently accepted him as he was. Terry sensed that the man, whom he had never met before, actually cared about him. At first Terry was threatened by the counselor's warmth but eventually accepted his sincerity and felt comfortable in his presence. After some time, he talked about his unusual feelings.

"You know, Mr. Caldwell, I didn't know what I was supposed to do when I came in here."

"I guess you were uncomfortable since you didn't know me before today," came the understanding reply.

"I figured this was kind of like going to the principal at school. Every time I have to go see an adult, I'm either in trouble or sick or something like that. I thought you were gonna yell at me or maybe spank me," explained the youngster. He laughed at his own lack of judgment.

"So you came in here expecting the worst from me."

"You know," Terry continued, "it's different with you. I think you trust me. I'll bet you're not even afraid that I'll tear your room up, are you?"

"I don't want to be afraid of you. I hope we can be friends. Sounds like that's a new experience for you," replied Mr. Caldwell.

"That's why my mother brought me here, isn't it? She doesn't trust me one bit. In fact, she doesn't even like me. She told me so. She says that she doesn't see how anyone could like me. I think that's how everyone feels about me," confided Terry.

"A lot of people have given you the feeling that you're no good. Nobody much cares for you."

"You know, I wish I could see you every day. We hit it off pretty good together." Terry was already buoyed by his encounter with someone who had a genuine interest in him.

"It feels good to know that someone else really cares for you, doesn't it, Terry?"

"Boy, I'll say! It's no good when everyone hates you."

Terry's mother had sought the assistance of a counselor because she believed he was a bad boy. In her own description of her son and their home setting, she stated that she and the boy's father tried to make sure that all of their children were clean and had everything they needed. They thought they were good parents and even told of how they remembered to buy Terry a birthday present every year. They were certain to punish him when he did wrong, but despite all of their efforts, they seemed to be unsuccessful in rearing Terry to be a wholesome child.

One of the primary ingredients missing in Terry's home was love! He could not know of his parents' love for him, for they had not told him by word or action. Much of his aggressive behavior signaled his unmet needs for love and acceptance. Much like Terry are many children, termed severe behavior problems, who fail to receive messages at home indicating that someone loves them and whose aggressive behavior is a reaction to a lack of complete acceptance by another person.

Those who have studied the human's emotional need for love have correctly informed us that the need takes on different forms throughout a lifetime. Small children tend to be more affectionate in a physical sense. They seek expressions of love in physical closeness, such as hugging or holding the hand of a parent. As they mature they seek love from others outside the immediate family in the form of recognition from peers, delighting in the knowledge that others understand and accept them. An adult seeks love that is intimate in nature. It is based on a mutual desire with another adult to both give of oneself to that person and receive what that person has to give in return. In most societies, the marriage contract is an expression of that need.

Throughout this book, a variety of ingredients that are necessary to create a healthy home atmosphere, along with discussions of behavior management methods and communication techniques, will be examined. But the important point here is that the child's need for love underscores everything else. Children who have not been hugged or kissed or even touched by a parent in recent memory, who have not been unconditionally valued first of all by their families, are not living in homes where they can develop caring attitudes. Parents need lots of help and encouragement in recognizing their children's value, emotional needs, and innate desires to be good and lovable, and in creating the atmosphere in which their children can flourish. It is the purpose of this book to provide some of that help.

*Children are an heritage of the LORD*
(Ps. 127:3 KJV).

# 3

# Turn Up the Thermostat!

Kenneth rushed in from baseball practice late one afternoon and found his father in the den reading the evening newspaper. "Hey, Dad! We learned something new at practice today!" he shouted excitedly.

Dad failed to look up. "Oh?"

"Coach Carlson is teaching us how to slide!"

"Yeah?" mumbled Dad.

"Yeah! We worked on sliding feet first, and he's even going to teach us how to slide head first—you know, like the pros do."

"I see," came the perfunctory reply. Dad wasn't really interested.

"I tried it. It's a blast sliding that way! It gets your uniform dirty, too. That makes you look like a real ballplayer."

"Huh?" said Dad, still engrossed in his newspaper.

"Never mind, Dad. Hey, Mom!" shouted Kenneth as he bounced off.

Brrr! The psychological atmosphere in Kenneth's house was cool—at least in the den where Dad was.

19

The expression of warmth is very similar to that of love. As we discussed in the previous chapter, all children behave in ways derived from their needs for love and acceptance from their parents. It is parents who play the greater role in the satisfaction of this basic need and they who provide the warm atmosphere in which love flourishes and children grow.

Studies conducted with infants show that, even though all other basic needs may be satisfactorily met, children who fail to receive physical warmth and love from their caretakers will likely suffer delays in their physical, mental, and emotional development. Children who lack warmth from their parents will have difficulty liking and respecting themselves, and will not be able to extend love and affection to others.

Like so many other attitudes and conditions, warmth is something that is not stated so much as it is expressed through actions. Warmth may be communicated from the parent to the child in the form of attention, tone of voice, emotional responsiveness to what the child is saying, eye contact, posture, and other nonverbal cues.

In the interaction between Kenneth and his father, Dad's lip service to what his son was saying to him was not sufficient to hide his lack of interest. He failed to focus on the boy and maintained a steady gaze on the newspaper. No facial expressions conveyed to Kenneth either a positive or negative emotion. Dad was nonverbally telling his son that he was too busy for him at the present time. He was not interested in promoting Kenneth's positive self-esteem. Kenneth correctly perceived the message that he was temporarily unimportant to his dad and immediately sought out his mother with the hope of locating a more promising source of warmth. With a series of communications between himself and his dad such as that one, Kenneth will come to see his father as distant to him and will in turn maintain a distance from him.

It was Saturday afternoon and the Spivey family was in their backyard playing a game of touch football. Fourteen-year-old Greg took the hike from his father. He looked for nine-year-old Jill and saw that she was in the open. Mother had been assigned to defend Jill. He tossed the football to his sister, and with open arms she made the catch and ran the ball for a touchdown.

Dad ran to meet Jill. "You caught it!" he exclaimed, sharing the excitement of his smiling daughter. At the same time, he reached out and tousled her hair. "That's the first catch I've made today, and it was a touchdown!" pronounced the pleased girl.

"I think you enjoyed that," replied Dad. "It's our turn to kick off."

Even in the context of backyard play, Jill's father had provided her with a sense of warmth. He had utilized a number of nonverbal cues to do so. Once Jill caught the ball, he ran to her side and touched her, placing the two family members in physical and psychological contact. No doubt there was a sparkle in his eyes and a sense of happiness about him similar to Jill's, his smile reflecting hers. By his words he acknowledged what she had accomplished. Without evaluating her action he allowed Jill to draw her own conclusions about what she had done.

Children cannot sense consistent feelings of warmth from their parents without a proper amount of attention. Most discussions of children's need for attention focus on the necessity of parents spending an adequate amount of time in the direct presence of their children on a daily basis. While this is certainly important, a word about the quality of the attention and warmth is also in order.

Mr. Walters had a rare weekday off and had a long list of things to do during the day. A light fixture in the living room needed repair, the gutters along the roof required cleaning, the garage was a mess and needed to be tidied, and so on. Since Mrs. Walters had her normally long list of daytime chores to be completed, she was glad to have her husband home to help her watch the children so she could get a good bit of work done, also. Five-year-old Sharon and three-year-old Karen had no plans but to play and tag along beside Mother and Daddy.

During the morning hours, Mother and Daddy were busily working inside the house. For a while the two girls entertained themselves in their room. Seeking some attention from their parents, they made their way into the living room and found Daddy fiddling with the lamp.

"What are you doing, Daddy?" inquired Karen.

"Fixing this lamp," he responded.

"Do you want to play blocks with me and Sharon?" came a request.

"Not now."

"When will you play?"

"Later, Karen. I want to fix this lamp," said Daddy, never making eye contact with either of the girls.

Sensing no warmth from Daddy, the girls hunted down Mother, who was in the dining room folding clothes. This time it was Sharon who sought her attention.

"We want you to play with us, Mommy," she stated.

"Not now. You can help me fold clothes, though," she offered.

"Okay!" Both girls were satisfied with their mother's offer. At least it provided them with the recognition they sought. Yet, no sooner had they begun to fold some towels when Mother picked up an armload of clothes and walked to another part of the house to store them away. The sisters simultaneously saw their chance to be noticed and receive positive attention vanish before them.

The remainder of the day continued in the same pattern. When one or both girls approached either parent, they got little attention and no sense of warmth or caring. The noontime meal was hurriedly prepared by Mrs. Walters who set the food on the kitchen counter, and everyone ate as they had time. In the afternoon the girls expressed boredom, but were merely told to play outdoors or watch television.

That evening at suppertime, Daddy looked around at his family. "I don't know about all of you, but this has been a good day for me. I really got a lot of much-needed work done."

At that, Mother added, "I've gotten a lot done today, too." Looking at her two daughters she added, "Thanks for being so good today. I'm sorry we didn't pay any more attention to you. We'll make it up another day."

Not surprisingly, neither girl showed much excitement at their mother's assurance. Her praise of the girls' good behavior was ineffective. It wasn't what the girls had sought nor what they needed. Despite the fact that Sharon and Karen had spent the entire day in the presence of their parents, they had felt no warmth. Sure, Mother and Daddy had been aware of their daughters and had spoken to them, but the quality of their attention had been poor—not negative but neutral—and damaging nevertheless.

*May the words of my mouth and
the meditation of my heart be
pleasing in your sight*
(Ps. 19:14 NIV).

# 4

# It's Not What You Say
# But How You Say It

While we may agree on the need for warmth in a healthy family atmosphere, it is easier to sense its presence or absence than to define it. Affectionate touching and quality attention are rather obvious manifestations of warmth. Closely akin is tone of voice. Although tone of voice is an element of communication and could well be discussed in part 3, its importance to a warm atmosphere merits our giving it attention here.

Many times a parent will say something to a child only to have the frustrating experience of having the child misinterpret what was said. Too often the intent of the words is lost somewhere in their transmission. On the other hand, parents may be totally oblivious to the impact of their messages, communicated through their tone of voice, or the development of their children's emotional well-being.

Shirley was helping her mother bake a cake. As they mixed the ingredients, Mother asked Shirley to measure out the flour. When the girl lifted the flour off the pantry shelf, she dropped the sack, and a good portion of it covered the floor.

"Oops! I dropped it!" exclaimed Shirley.

"Yes, you *dropped* it," retorted Mother with emphasis.

Shirley felt embarrassed. "It was a mistake."

"Mm, hmm," was all she heard.

In this brief exchange, Mother actually only spoke a handful of words, but she certainly said a lot. Through her tone of voice and facial expressions she told Shirley what she thought of her. The heaviness with which she stated, "Yes, you *dropped* it," not only conveyed her acknowledgment of what had happened but also her judgment. Shirley had done a foolish, even disgusting thing in Mother's estimation. There is no doubt that Mother's pronouncement brought on or at the very least enhanced Shirley's embarrassment.

Mother's reply to Shirley's apology did little to soften the blow of her first response. In muttering "Mm, hmm" Mother sent the message that she was uninterested in the girl's feelings. Rather, Mother was focusing her concern on the actual event and the mess that had been made. In effect, she turned a cold shoulder to her daughter and failed to show warmth, understanding, or compassion.

A child's self-concept is largely developed on the basis of feedback from others. Much of what we believe about the inherent goodness of our children is communicated by the way we speak to them. There must be consistency in the verbal and nonverbal communications children receive from their parents. These uniform communications give children clear messages. They know exactly how their parents feel about them.

Neal had played on baseball teams since Little League days. Now he had earned a starting position on his high school's team. His parents attended many of his games and were proud of their son, even though he was not the star of the team. One evening after a winning team effort,

Neal and his family sat in their home. The subject of the day's game naturally came up.

"I guess you were pleased that you beat City High today. That win put your team in contention for the league title," commented Dad.

"Yeah, I'm glad we won. I just wish I had contributed a little more to the win, though. I didn't even get a hit today." Neal sighed.

"Not getting a hit took some fun out of winning, I guess."

"Yeah, I'm glad we won. I just wish I had contributed a little more to the win, though. I didn't even get a hit today." Neal sighed.

"You know, I wouldn't say you didn't make a contribution today, though. You did well in the fifth inning when you walked and stole second base. Then you scored on Henry's base hit. That run was an important run for your team," recalled Dad. There was encouragement in his voice.

Neal spoke more enthusiastically. "Coach Woodrow did mention that run to me after the game. At least I did one thing that was helpful today."

In this conversation, Neal's dad had averted the possibility of his son dwelling on his faults as a baseball player. Instead, Dad provided a psychological "shot in the arm" to Neal when he needed it. Dad did not focus only on what his son had done wrong, which was what Neal was doing. He reminded his son of his positive action during the game and spoke of it in a voice of pride and hopefulness. Notice that Dad did acknowledge what Neal pointed out, that the youth had failed to get a hit that day, but he refrained from pronouncing judgment on his son or telling him that he expected more hits in the next game.

From that communication Neal came away with a feeling that his dad believed in him as a person. At least his dad would accept him as he was, hitless or not. In effect, his father had told him in various ways, "You are a person who has worth." Neal received that message loud and clear.

One of the most difficult circumstances many parents face with their children arises when the parents feel a need or desire to turn down their children's requests. In doing so, it is difficult to avoid communicating rejection. The tone of voice that is chosen by a parent can either foster a resulting hurt or be used to avoid such an occurrence.

Mr. Harrison had an especially busy day at work. His boss had asked him to complete an important project by the end of the day, causing him to work a little longer than usual. He had barely had time to gobble down a bit of lunch and had relaxed only a few minutes the entire day. As he walked into the house, his six-year-old daughter, Jenny, met him at the door.

"Daddy! I've been waiting for you! One of the pedals on my bike came off this afternoon. Would you please put it back on?"

Mr. Harrison looked down at his daughter. He thought to himself that a demanding daughter was the last thing he wanted to contend with right then.

"I'm tired," he grumbled. "I've had a rough day at the office! *Maybe* I'll feel like it after supper," he added, with little promise in his voice.

At that, Jenny sought out her older brother and warned him, "Stay away from him. He's Oscar the Grouch tonight."

That was one way it could have happened. Now, imagine the same situation, the same tired father, the same eagerly awaiting daughter, but notice in the following retelling the changed atmosphere with the father's changed tone of voice.

"Daddy! I've been waiting for you! One of the pedals on my bike came off this afternoon. Would you please put it back on?"

Mr. Harrison sensed his daughter was counting on him to provide aid in a job she could not do. He really wanted to help, but he also wanted a few minutes to unwind from the day's activities.

"I'm tired," he said softly as he bent down and hugged his child, nonverbally communicating that he was glad to see her. "I've had a rough day at the office," he confided to her. "Maybe I'll feel like it after supper," he added, winking at her.

Jenny sought out her brother with a different message. "Be nice to Daddy tonight. This has been a bad day, and he needs some peace and quiet."

The wording was exactly the same in both versions of the exchange. The difference in the messages and the atmosphere was that Mr. Harrison handled his end of the conversation with a different tone of voice. In the first example, he told Jenny (whether he realized it or not), "I'm in a foul mood. Everything has gone against me today. I'm not interested in you, and I'm certainly not interested in your broken bicycle." Not only had he dampened relations between himself and his child, he had also created a chasm between the two of them. Also, through his daughter's warning to her brother, he indirectly told his son that the same message applied to him. You can imagine that Jenny would not need to receive many similar messages to get the feeling that her father didn't think a great deal of her worth. Neither would he be the one to turn to when a need for warmth or love and affection arose. There was not a psychologically healthy atmosphere there.

On the other hand, by the way he stated the same words in the second story, Mr. Harrison handed his daughter an opposite set of messages. He was receptive to her delight in seeing him. He recognized her confidence that her dad could repair the pedal on her crippled bicycle. Because he was exhausted from a long day at work, however, he wanted a few minutes to himself. Through the words he spoke and the way in which he spoke them, he communicated to Jenny, "I'm glad I can tell you how I really feel right now. I know you'll understand." He also sent the message, "You're important to me. Therefore, I'll be glad to fix your bike after I've had the chance to relax." Jenny walked away from that brief exchange with her father satisfied that he would provide the assistance she needed. She also had an increased sense of self-worth, because her father had conveyed to her that she mattered to him. By the different tone of his voice, Mr. Harrison made the experience positive. He showed respect for his daughter through his warmth, and taught Jenny, in an indirect manner, the importance of considering the needs of others—a lesson she shared with her brother.

Finally, a word about courtesy. How often have you witnessed scenes in which parents talked to their own children in tones of resentment, sarcasm, or even downright hatred? Do you think that most adults would speak to a stranger's children in the same way? Of course not! They would be more polite, especially if the children were accompanied by one or both parents. If parents, then, are able to talk in respectful tones to other people's children, why shouldn't they give their own children the same consideration?

Four-year-old Camille and her neighborhood playmate, Ellen, were playing in Camille's front yard. Her mother glanced out the window to check on the girls and saw both of them stepping out into the street to chase a ball. Mother rushed to the front porch. "Camille! You get out of the street right now! Do you hear me?" There was no uncertainty in her voice that she was angry. Then, turning her attention to Ellen, she sweetly urged, "Ellen, stay out of the street, dear. I know your mother would not want you to go into the street without an adult." Both girls obeyed the command, but as they walked back into the yard, Camille began to cry while Ellen merely looked on.

Camille's mother made a basic error in the harsh tone

of voice she used with her daughter. To make matters worse, she switched to her polite tone of voice, speaking more gently to Ellen. Why did Camille cry? She was hurt! Mother was, in essence, saying that Camille was not as worthy of courtesy as was her guest.

Tone of voice sets the stage for a host of messages to follow. Parents who consistently use a calm speaking voice, do not talk condescendingly, do carry hints of encouragement and enthusiasm in their voices, and speak courteously to their children are following an effective rule of thumb: speak to children as though they are welcomed friends with whom you wish to have a healthy and meaningful relationship. Your tone of voice will set the atmosphere for making your wish come true.

*Test everything.*
*Hold on to the good*
(1 THESS. 5:21 NIV).

# 5

# Create an Atmosphere
# Which Allows Experiment

Dad was mowing the yard as he routinely did on Saturday morning. Eight-year-old Sam sat on the porch admiring his father's work. He thought to himself that it must be wonderful to be able to operate a lawnmower the way his dad did. He had tried it before and would really like to try it again. With a burst of excitement, he made his way to his dad's side.

"Dad," he shouted, trying to talk over the noise of the mower. "I've got a great idea!"

Dad paused. He'd heard that line before. "What is it this time?" he inquired.

"Why don't you sit on the porch for a while while I mow the grass?"

Dad looked down at his son, who was wearing a broad smile, and reluctantly agreed. He knew that Sam did not know how to mow grass very well. He always left strips of grass untouched, and sometimes cut down things that should be left standing.

As he sat on the steps of the porch, Dad could not

31

refrain from shouting instructions to his son. "You've already mowed that spot. Keep your lines straight. Watch out for the flowers. Turn the throttle down!"

Sam had mowed no more than a few strips of grass before turning the task back to his father. "It wasn't as much fun as I thought it would be," he moaned as he walked into the house.

Sam's dad was confused. He could not figure out what had caused Sam to become dejected so suddenly. After all, he did agree to let the boy do something that he considered "grown up."

Actually, Sam was *not* provided the opportunity to experiment and discover what it was like to be grown up, which was what he wanted to do. Everything he did seemed to be wrong. He had not mowed in a straight line, did not know a flower from a blade of grass, and was at fault because the lawnmower was so loud. In effect his dad let him know he had failed in his job.

The messages a parent sends his child in the form of either encouragement or discouragement come through as loudly as if they were shouted through a megaphone. Let's analyze the messages Sam received in the course of a few brief moments.

Sam received only a tentative vote of confidence when his dad reluctantly agreed to allow him to mow the grass. Through his father's directives from the porch, Sam surmised that he was not capable of doing the job on his own, used poor judgment, and was a failure in his experiment with a new situation.

Suppose we change the scenario a bit. Suppose that, in this instance, Sam's dad allowed his son to mow for a five-minute period while he rested on the porch. At the end of the designated time, he stopped his son, who was becoming weary by then, and asked, "Well, Sam, how'd it go?"

Sam replied, "It was harder work than I thought, but it sure was fun! Maybe I'll relieve you again and try to work for ten minutes the next time." He then trotted into the house to get a refreshment and to tell his little brother how he had contributed to doing the day's chores.

In this instance, Sam received an entirely different set of messages from his dad and was able to make more positive inferences about his own worth as a human being. His father's willingness to enter into a working partnership with him conveyed trust and encouragement. The fact that his dad sat quietly on the porch while Sam toiled allowed the youngster to discover for himself what it was like to be involved in a physically demanding task. The lack of criticism and constant instructions from Dad told Sam that he was a boy who was capable of making his own decisions and coming to his own conclusions about the work he had done. The lad who walked into the house to tell his brother of his achievement was more fulfilled and had more of a sense of self-worth than the one who sulked as he left his dad, feeling as if he were a failure.

In the second instance, as in the first, Dad may have seen minor damage to his well-groomed lawn, but he had taken advantage of an opportunity to create an atmosphere of encouragement. He correctly recognized that a yard of grass can be reconditioned far more easily than the life of his child.

A well-known psychologist, Eric Erickson, has worked out a theory of human personality development. He sees the human individual as being in a continuous state of change and development throughout the entire life cycle. He identifies the eight stages of life through which all men and women progress. Five of these stages take place during the childhood and adolescent years. People are always interacting with their environment, rather than passively watching life wander by.

Early in children's lives, well before entering the "educational years" of school, they develop their attitudes toward the world. It is a place where significant persons can either be trusted or viewed with suspicion. As they grow older children increasingly interact with their world. During this time parents exert a powerful influence: either they encourage broadening experiences or discourage their children's developing security with their world.

Children are in a precarious position by being physically smaller than adults. As a result, children have a natural tendency to place great value on adults, especially parent figures. Parents who downgrade, criticize, or persistently supervise their children as they interact with their environment are more likely to rear timid or dejected children who doubt their own capabilities to act independently. In the first example of this chapter, Sam's dad squelched his son's natural wonder about the joys in the simple task of mowing the lawn. He did not encourage Sam to experiment independently with his environment.

Sid was an eight-year-old in the second grade. He was an average student whose behavior at school was usually within acceptable limits. On this particular day, however, Sid had stepped outside those limits and was now his own messenger of doom. As he walked home, he clutched a handwritten note from his teacher to his parents. In the note was a description of his determination to learn about the fish in the fish tank in the classroom. The note explained that, although Sid was aware of the classroom rule forbidding students to place their hands in the fish's water, he had become so enamoured with the scaly creatures that he had reached into the tank in an attempt to catch a fish for a closer look. In the process, he had accidentally spilled water on the classroom floor, not to mention his pants and Wesley Baker's tennis shoes. None of the fish had been harmed, although they certainly had been frightened quite a bit.

Sid was not enthusiastic as he walked into his house to deliver the note to Mother. She greeted him at the door.

"Hi, Sid. How was school?" Sid said nothing, but handed his mother the note. He stood silently, with head hung low, while she read of his doings.

"How did this happen, Sid? This isn't like you. You know I'm disappointed in you. I can't believe you would do something like this. You should know you can't reach in the fish tank and catch a fish. I certainly hope that you've learned a lesson about your bad behavior. You can bet that when Daddy gets home we'll talk about this some more."

Sid dreaded his father's arrival at home that evening. As she had promised, within minutes after Daddy came into the house, Mother summoned Sid into their presence and handed his father the note.

"I want you to read this note and see for yourself what our son has done today." Dad took the note and began reading it. Before he had read past the first few words, Mother directed a few comments toward her son.

"I hope you realize how ashamed this incident makes me. It hurts to know that you would create such a mess in your classroom. The next thing you know, we're going to be called to your school to take you home because of something naughty you've done. I'll bet none of the other children in your class stuck their arm down in the fish tank. What do you have to say for yourself?"

"I was just trying to see what the fish felt like . . ."

"What the fish felt like!" interrupted Mother. "It feels rough and smells bad. That's what a fish is like! Sid, you can't keep on doing this type of thing at school. I'm sorry, but you may not play outside for the rest of the week."

With that pronouncement, she stood like a stone and looked sternly at Sid, as Daddy stood by saying nothing. Sid walked from the room with his head hung low, feeling as if he had just been sentenced to twenty years behind bars.

Shame, shame! The message from Mother to son was clear. Sid was a boy with normal curiosity about something in his environment—the fish in the tank at school.

Although he probably realized the impropriety of sticking his hand into a fish tank, he decided to take a risk for the sake of experimentation, attempted to catch a fish so that he could handle it and examine it in a novel way.

While we probably would agree that Sid needed to be talked to about the manner of his seeking information, we would also agree that the tongue lashing he received from his mother was unnecessary. Not only did she fail to focus on the specific misbehavior (breaking a classroom rule), but under the guise of her own hurt pride she effectively conveyed her disapproval of his need to experiment.

Erickson tells us that young children develop an autonomy for dealing effectively with their environment. They have a natural tendency to explore the environment, to try out new forms of behavior, and to learn all they can about their world. This experimental nature is most evident in preschool-aged children, but continues throughout childhood and into adulthood.

In providing children the appropriate atmosphere for growth, we must make allowances for their experimental nature. Children whose parents thwart their natural curiosity will develop doubt—doubt about both their world and themselves. In the case of Sid, a sense of shame was the result of the uncompromising scrutiny of his mother. He had received an evaluation of his experimental behavior and was given a failing grade. He had not been provided the opportunity to undergo a self-evaluation, but instead experienced an intense sense of guilt.

Parents who downgrade and belittle their children's behavior will produce a sense of worthlessness in them and cause them to believe that little they do has any redeeming value. Sam's father fostered Sam's negative feeling by showing impatience while he performed a new task. Sid's mother caused him to feel badly about himself by dwelling on a relatively small error in judgment and showering him with shame.

Children choose different ways to react to the controlling ways of their parents. One may become outwardly defiant and hostile, another excessively conforming and timid. Still another may become rigid and overly concerned with maintaining a fixed, safe routine. All have one common denominator. They have learned that experimentation in their environment is unsafe. The potential harm to their sense of self-worth and their effectiveness as creative human beings is too great to risk such a loss.

*The Duty of Parents to their*
*children . . . is to be tender-hearted,*
*pitiful [compassionate] and gentle.*
JEREMY TAYLOR

# 6

# Gimme a Little Respect

A well-known comedian is famous for his constant complaint that he gets no respect. Many children may feel justified in making this same accusation of their parents: they get no respect. But respect is a prerequisite for encouraging a child's growth.

For Phil's tenth birthday his parents gave him a bicycle. Because his son enjoyed working with his hands and tinkering with mechanical objects, Dad thought it would be a fun and rewarding experience for the two of them to assemble the bike together in a team effort. The task progressed rapidly and smoothly, and they soon found themselves putting the reflector lights in place and nearing completion of the project.

"Dad," queried Phil, "since you've done most of the work on the bike, maybe could I put the reflectors on by myself?"

"That's a good idea, son," came the reply. Phil reached for a screw, a washer, and a nut, preparing to mount the first reflector.

"That nut won't fit the screw, son. Let me find one that will." As Phil looked on, Dad fished through his tool box until he found a nut that matched the screw. "Here's one, Bud."

"Thanks, Dad." Phil put the washer and nut into place. After twisting the screw as far as he could with his fingers, he reached for a screwdriver.

"You need a phillip's head screwdriver, Phil, not a flat one."

"Oh, yeah, I see." He reached for the correct tool and proceeded to tighten the screw.

"Do you have it tight enough? Let me see," commented Dad as he reached over to test his son's work. "Perhaps a little tighter."

Upon completion of the task, Dad beamed at his son. "There, you did it! That's a job well-done, too."

"Yeah, I guess," stated Phil flatly. "I could have done it by myself, you know."

On the surface it seemed that Phil's dad had done little wrong; nevertheless, he was all but rejected by his son. What he did not realize, however, was that he had not shown a great deal of respect to the boy who was trying out a relatively new skill. For example, in pointing out that the nut would not fit the screw he doubted Phil's ability to select the right one. Phil certainly noticed that he needed to select another nut. Similarly, by offering advice to tighten the screw Dad suggested that Phil was unable to complete the job on his own satisfactorily. Phil's expectation of doing a task on his own vanished. Dad dispelled Phil's belief that he could do something without relying on the resources of others.

What is meant by the term *respect*? I am referring to parents' responses to children that show trust in the youngsters' ability to handle most situations appropriately. Respect is often shown more by what parents refrain from doing for children than in what they actually do.

Parents who respect their children hold a strong belief that children have the potential for growth, and are willing to allow their children to experiment. Of course, we all know that children cannot do all things for themselves, but respectful parents will refrain from habitually intervening in their children's efforts and will trust them to ask for help at the appropriate time.

Alice was two and one-half years old and was learning to dress herself. "Mommy, I want to put my pants on by myself," she announced one morning. Mother consented, handing her daughter's pants to her. Alice sat on the floor and laid the trousers in front of her. She put her right leg in the pants properly, and then proceeded to shove her left leg into the same opening. Mother sat on the edge of the bed, patiently watching with interest. Alice attempted to stand, but immediately plopped to the carpet. Realizing her error, she pulled out her misplaced leg, slipped it into the correct spot, and stood tall. After hoisting her britches to the waistline, she looked at her mother and smiled.

"Look, Mommy, I did it! Would you snap these? I can't."

"I can see you're proud of yourself, Alice," replied Mother as she fastened the snap.

Although Alice had made errors in putting on her pants, Mother allowed her to discover her mistakes on her own. She said nothing discouraging or suggestive of lack of trust in Alice's ability to handle the task. Simply put, Mother respected Alice's efforts. Because her mother has a healthy respect for her, Alice will come to respect herself and will strive to become an independent girl.

Too often, as parents we attempt to impose our own set of beliefs and thoughts onto our children and give them little chance to express themselves. They may wish they had never spoken to us.

Ray and his brother, Ricky, shared a bedroom. Of the two, Ray was the one most concerned about neatness.

He kept his clothes hung in the closet, put away his shoes and socks, and kept his toys in place when not in use. Ricky, on the other hand, was less interested in the appearance of the room. His dirty socks were frequently scattered about, and he often forgot to put away toys and games. One day, Ray became especially exasperated with Ricky and told his mother of his frustrations.

"Mother, I've picked up my things in our bedroom, but it still doesn't look very clean. Rick left all of his clothes and toys on the floor."

"So what difference does that make?" came the reply. "You take care of your things and leave Ricky's things for him to pick up. I don't know why you're so worried about Ricky's mess."

"But Mother, you don't understand! I worked hard to make our room look nice and then Ricky came in and messed it all up. You can't even tell that I've done any work in our room. I just wanted it to look nice."

"Oh, Ray, I don't think things are quite as bad as they seem. Don't worry about it so much. Ricky will get around to picking up his things eventually; he always does."

Following this fruitless discussion Ray walked to his room and pouted. As he surveyed the untidy room, he could not help but think that no one seemed to care about his feelings nor understand his frustration. Deep within him was resentment toward both his mother and Ricky. They failed to respect his desire to keep his bedroom neatly arranged.

Ray was correct in his thinking. Mother did not respect his thoughts and feelings and communicated as much to her son. Rather than take his complaint seriously, she devalued his feelings and communicated to him that she did not wish to invest herself in him and his concerns.

When Ray first approached Mother, her response was, "What difference does it make?" Such a statement did little to encourage Ray to think he was going to receive any degree of respect from his mother. Mother might as well have stated, "I don't care what your room looks like, and neither should you." She revealed a lack of commitment to him. It is no wonder that the boy felt resentment as he walked to his bedroom and once again surveyed the untidy conditions.

Respect for a child involves openness and a willingness to become invested in the child's world. Rather than hearing messages such as "what difference does it make" or "it can't be that bad," the child needs to know that what he says will be taken seriously by his parents.

How could Ray's mother have shown respect to him when he approached her regarding the untidy bedroom? She could have initially responded by saying, "So you feel that Ricky is not being fair to you. After you clean up the room, Ricky comes in and puts clothes and toys all around the room. That must be frustrating to you."

Such a response would indicate to Ray that she identified with his frustration, understood the reasons behind his emotions, and would invest herself in the situation because she realized its importance to her son. Because Mother would have refused to take sides, Ray would know that Ricky, too, would be treated respectfully and nonjudgmentally. Mother's respect would have increased the likelihood of reaching an acceptable resolution to Ray's problem.

In an atmosphere where self-respect, a respect for others, and a sense of responsibility are fostered, children learn that people have value and in turn become committed to and involved in the thoughts and feelings of others.

Overprotection, although it may appear opposite on the surface, is lack of respect in the extreme.

Two neighborhood boys rang the front doorbell. Mrs. Ellis opened the door. "Hi, boys. What do you need?"

"We need Earl. We're trying to find enough kids for a good game of hide and seek."

Earl heard his friends' voices and headed out the door. "Is it okay if I play, Mother?" he asked, anticipating an affirmative response.

"Just a moment, fella. It's getting cool. Come in and get a sweater."

Earl noticed that his companions did not wear sweaters, but did as his mother told him. Quickly he returned, pulling on his sweater. "See ya later," he said over his shoulder.

"Earl, your shoe is untied. Don't leave until you've tied it. Also, be in the house in half an hour."

Earl muttered as he stooped and tied his shoelaces. Then came another question. "Who else will be playing with you? I don't want you getting dirty."

"Oh, Mother, I'll be all right. Can I go now? They're waiting." He then managed to slip away as his mother looked on to make sure he made his way safely.

Mrs. Ellis would likely be shocked to know that by hovering too closely over Earl she conveyed a lack of respect or trust in him and created an unhealthy atmosphere for his growth.

The child who is under the umbrella of an overly protective parent learns that the world is an unsafe place and dares not explore that world. Shying away from experimentation leaves the child with a short-sighted view of life.

Such children are told they are not capable of making their own decisions: adults must make decisions for them. While few would admit it, there are parents who actually prefer to follow this guideline, unable to face the growing independence of that baby they once rocked in a cradle. Deep down, these parents believe their children really are *not* able to make responsible decisions on their own and must be controlled.

It is true that direction must be given to all children,

with more direction required at different chronological and developmental ages. Children of all ages must also, however, be subjected to the natural consequences of their own behavior. They will learn far more through experimental interaction with their environment than from the lips of others. Indeed, some lessons are taught solely by experience.

Children who are hovered over generally develop low self-esteem. Because they are told in one way or another that the world is unsafe, that they are poor decision makers and not responsible for their actions, they eventually come to believe they don't have much going for themselves and must be psychological weaklings.

There are two routes over-protected children may choose, and neither is desirable in the long run. First, they may believe their parents' messages and become helpless persons who must rely on sources outside themselves for strength. Of course, in many cases that source of strength continues to be their parents.

When such children reach adulthood, they often emerge as troubled or troublesome marriage partners. They are unable to make decisions or take responsibility for their actions. They may be men who are extremely fastidious, very demanding of their wives, or expect their wives to be extensions of their mothers. They may be dependent women who cling to their husbands for protection or identity, or keep returning home to Mama.

The other route that overly protected children may take is rebellion. As children grow older and see the independence and autonomy many of their peers have, they may develop deep resentment of their parents. Even while they continue to receive messages from one or both parents that they are incapable of making proper decisions and are psychological weaklings, they reject those ideas and refuse to believe they require their parents' constant care and guidance. In a figurative sense, and possibly in a literal sense, they run away from their smothering parents. They often assert their independence as mouthy teenagers, seek more-than-usual companionship with peers away from home, and finally leave home and family contact altogether.

Children not only do not want to be protected from the consequences of their own behavior, they also do not need to be protected. They have the natural desire to explore their world, to learn from it, and to live with what they find. The role of parents is to guide children to seek answers rather than assume they must be given immediate answers to all of life's questions. Parents must provide challenges that stimulate children toward growth and learning and carefully allow children to make their own judgments, even though in the short term they may be doomed to failure, and to learn from the consequences.

*Everyone should be respected as an
individual, but no one idolized.*
ALBERT EINSTEIN

# 7

# Be Democratic
# in Decision Making

It was suppertime at the Lawrence house. The normal routine of gathering the family together for the evening meal had taken place.

"Mom," inquired Beth, "I wanted to watch that special program on TV, and it's time for it to begin. Do I have to eat supper in the dining room with everybody else?"

Mom felt as though she had been put on the spot. It was an unwritten rule in their family that the evening meal would be eaten together. That was the one time of day in which the entire family could be corralled into one room. She knew, however, that Beth had been looking forward to viewing a special children's program. Should she sacrifice the family's time of togetherness so Beth could watch the show, or insist on maintaining the normal routine?

"I see that the TV program is on at the same time as our mealtime," was Mom's reply. "That presents a dilemma."

A conversation ensued among the family members,

with the decision being to eat in the den on TV trays. It provided a change of pace, allowed the family to enjoy a time together, and caused no ill feelings. A democratic process had been followed and an agreement reached that was satisfactory to all concerned.

Too many parents take upon themselves the role of dictator and squelch mutual respect and encouragement within the home. A dictator-parent makes the rules, gives commands, and decides on important (and even unimportant) matters. The child is placed in the role of "subject," he is expected to follow the imposed rules and directions, and show respect to the dictator. This is hardly an environment that fosters growth.

I'm not advocating that the role of the parent is to be a complete reverse of that mentioned above. The family certainly needs the leadership that parents can provide. Rather, the family unit can and should be a microcosm of the ideal democratic society. The parents are in the position of leadership, albeit not by virtue of a vote. The children represent the "grass roots" constituency for whom policies are made. While the parents are in a natural position of authority, it is their responsibility to solicit suggestions and comments of all family members so that the decisions are most beneficial to the family as a whole.

A wise political leader gets out among the constituents to "feel their heart's pulse" in an effort to take responsible action on their desires. Parents are in an ideal position to perform this very same function. They meet their "constituents" in the privacy of their own homes and discuss with them their concerns.

Fifteen-year-old Robert several times in recent weeks had gone on outings with some of his friends and was out rather late at night—a situation that caused his parents discomfort. In each instance he was supervised by adults and not in real danger of getting in trouble. Robert's thirteen-year-old brother, Roy, however, had noticed Robert's freedom and the exceptions that had been made in allowing him to keep the late hours. He wanted a slice of the pie!

Perceiving the potential controversy, the parents decided to meet with their sons for a conference. "Something's been on my mind," Dad announced. "The past few weeks we've let Robert stay out later than usual several times. I'm wondering if that's caused any problems for anyone."

Roy spoke first. "Well, Dad, I wish you'd let me do as many fun things as Robert gets to do."

Robert retorted, "Yeah, but you're a lot younger. You shouldn't get to stay out as late as I do."

Mother said, "It seems that the main problem is that Roy feels he should have the freedom that Robert enjoys, but Robert feels justified in what he does because he is two years older."

Dad spoke again, "Before this becomes a major problem, boys, I'd like you to suggest what we might do about this predicament."

Several possible solutions were offered, ranging from providing equal rights to both boys to stripping both boys of any freedom at all. All suggestions were discussed, some in more detail than others, and after several minutes, a satisfactory "settlement" had been reached: Roy's Friday-night privileges were extended for late bedtime and having friends over, and Robert understood he was not to take liberties with his privileges.

As the wise leaders of the family, Mother and Dad had recognized a potential problem between their "constituents"—Robert and Roy—whom they respected. They called a meeting, and with input from the entire family, arrived at a democratic solution.

Several important outgrowths of such a family conference are evident. First, guidelines for future behavior were set. Questions regarding Robert's and Roy's outside activities would henceforth be answered on the basis of the decision all family members had helped make earlier at the conference. No one could correctly claim that another family member was being treated preferentially or being "ganged up" on. As in any model democratic society, if problems arise concerning the original agreement (and they will), modifications can be made by holding another conference. In this way, experimentation is rendered safe.

Second, by entering into a conference with their children, parents create a sense of trust in the home. Many siblings prefer to "slug it out" when a problem arises, because they know that if the matter is brought before Mom or Dad a judgment will be rendered and probably neither child will win out. However, in an atmosphere that is democratic, no problem is unsolvable. In it all family members feel that their points of view will be heard and respected. Cooperation, trust in one another, and a willingness to compromise are encouraged.

Finally, and perhaps most importantly, children will apply the experience they have had at home to other situations. The parents have provided a model for dealing effectively with others when strife is present. Because the message has been conveyed that all people's feelings and opinions are important and worthy of consideration, the children will imitate this trust and view others in the same manner.

*Blessed are the peacemakers*
(MATT. 5:9 RSV).

# 8

# Peace Talks, Not Battle Lines

Parents and children spend a great deal of time under the same roof and know one another in ways that even the closest of friends are unaware. At home both parents and children let down their hair, so to speak. They say and do things that would be considered taboo in public. People show different sides of themselves at home than in public. A girl who wouldn't dare talk back to a teacher frequently challenges her parents at home. The boy known as the sweetest kid on the block can be quite a sourpuss at home. At home children frequently feel brave enough to invite their parents to go to battle, but with forethought the battles can be avoided or contained. Peace talks rather than battle lines can be laid as the norm in the house.

"Molly, would you *please* be still," requested an exasperated Mrs. Madison to her eight-year-old daughter. "I'm trying to fix your hair."

"But, Mom, it hurts. You're pulling my hair," whined Molly.

"Your hair won't look pretty if you don't let me fix it," came the reply. Mrs. Madison took pride in the compliments her daughter received on her impeccable looks. She tried to ensure that her little girl looked as nice as possible in public.

"Mom, how much longer? It hurts!"

Mr. Madison felt that his right to a quiet household had been infringed upon—again. "Would you two stop that constant bickering? That's all I hear every morning when I get up," he said.

Probably every parent has had a similar experience. On the surface it is a situation that is difficult to resolve. Mrs. Madison wants her daughter to have well-groomed hair and is willing to spend a few minutes each morning primping her daughter. On the other hand, Molly wiggles and squirms and generally makes her mother's job much more difficult than necessary.

The whole ordeal could be avoided, however. Mrs. Madison sets the scene for a small battle and gets one. By requiring her eight-year-old to sit still for several minutes to have her hair combed and braided, Mrs. Madison asks the child to do something that is difficult for her. She puts Molly in a precarious situation in which the odds of winning her full cooperation are slim, and the chances they will end up in a fight are pretty high.

What choices does Mrs. Madison have in the matter? In the first place, it is not absolutely necessary that Molly's hair be put into braids. A simpler hair style could suffice. Mrs. Madison is fulfilling her own desires to have a daughter who appears in public looking stylish. Molly has not requested this hair style. Mrs. Madison could avoid the battle entirely by not walking onto the battlefield.

If Mrs. Madison chooses to reject the option of grooming her daughter's hair in a different, simpler manner, she can now anticipate certain problems and complaints from her resistant daughter and be ready to deal with them. In that way, whining and complaining from Molly can be met by a calm, prepared mother who is stepping onto the battlefield backed by a rational plan of action. While the former plan (avoiding battles) is preferable to the latter (preparing for battles), circumstances frequently arise in family life that must be confronted with rational, peaceful plans of action.

While there are parents' actions that invite children to battle, there are also frequent invitations issued by children to parents to engage in warfare. In fact, many parents would insist that another World War is constantly on the verge of eruption in their home!

In the Hardin household, one of the values Mother held was that of fairness and equality. It was her opinion that responsibility and any family-related tasks should be shared by everyone. One of her rules was that following supper, each member of the family was to place his or her dishes in the dishwasher. It was considered by all members of the family to be a fair and reasonable request. Mother was rather perturbed, however, at Tim's regular bout of forgetfulness and frequent need to be reminded to take care of his dishes. The problem finally came to a head one evening.

"Tim, you forgot to take your dishes again. Get back here and do it now!" demanded Mother.

"Mother, I'm tired of having to do that. I don't want to anymore."

"You get back here *right now*, young man, and do as you are told!"

Tim ignored his mother's command and walked toward his bedroom.

"I said *now!*" reaffirmed Mother, who was getting angry at her son's resistance.

Tim had engaged his mother in a conflict and was determined to win this one as a matter of principle. He strolled back into the kitchen and stood his ground.

"Mother, I get tired of picking up my dishes every night. Can't you do it?"

Following an exchange of words and a series of threats by Mrs. Hardin, the conflict ended. Tim begrudgingly stacked his dishes. Although his mother had beat him this time, he would have other chances to win—chances he was sure to take advantage of.

Actually, in this incident there was no winner in the struggle for supremacy between Tim and his mother. An unhealthy atmosphere had been established in their home and seemed destined to become more unpleasant. In his refusal to carry out his assigned duty, one which was reasonable and fair, Tim invited his mother to do battle. A wise Mrs. Hardin would have refused such an invitation. Through word and deed she could communicate to her son that fighting was not her method for solving problem situations.

On receiving Tim's words that he did not want to place his dishes in the dishwasher (the invitation), Mrs. Hardin should have sent a notice of "regret," so to speak, that the invitation must be turned away.

"Tim," she might have said, "I don't want to argue about a small point such as that. You know the rules in this house. Once you've finished your meal, you must take your dishes away from the table. If you choose to leave them, I will assume that you're not interested in taking part in our regular dinner routine and will not set a place at the table for you tomorrow evening."

In the likelihood that Tim retaliated by resisting Mother's statement (a re-issuance of the original invitation), Mother should once again refuse his offer.

"That's the way it will be, son. It's up to you to decide what you will do."

By changing her reaction to Tim's oppositional behavior, Mrs. Hardin would have avoided a conflict with her son and maintained an atmosphere of fairness and respect. In the first instance, she attempted to solve

Tim's problem for him by forcing him to comply with the household rule. She placed herself in a precarious position, for if she won the battle by making him take care of his dishes, she failed to place the choice and the responsibility for making the choice on him. If she lost the battle, she knew that others would follow, for Tim would see her as an easy mark and would attempt to win other concessions through similar tactics.

One of the most difficult things for parents is to recognize attempts by children to engage them in power struggles and to calmly offer the children sets of choices. Of course, once children have chosen their option, the parents must follow through, in a calm manner, with their end of the agreement. Thus parents are in essence saying, "You're too important a person for me to spend my time bickering with you. I prefer that you make your own decisions on certain matters and I will offer you guidance in telling you what options are available. I do not want our home to be characterized by chaos, but I want us to maintain a calm, rational atmosphere."

While many invitations from children to enter into conflict are blatant and easily recognizable, others are more subtle. A child may shield an underlying desire for dominance by innocence and even charm.

Vicki had been in bed for thirty minutes and remained awake. "Mom," she called out, "I need to go to the bathroom."

Mom sighed to herself. This request was Vicki's third since going to bed. Each request had required attention. Soon after she had bedded down, Vicki had asked for a dose of cough syrup to curb her nagging cough. A few minutes later she complained of itching mosquito bites that required care. Now she needed to use the bathroom. "Go ahead," replied Mom in a stern voice, "but make it fast. You need to go to sleep. You have school tomorrow."

Following her trip to the bathroom, Vicki climbed into

bed. After five minutes, she called out again. "Mom, my mosquito bites still itch."

Mom was disgusted by now. "Vicki, we've already tended to those. Get to sleep—*now!*"

"But Mom . . ."

"Now!"

Vicki sobbed for a short time and complained to herself for a moment, but was soon fast asleep. Mom contemplated how she could go about stopping this regular pattern of behavior.

While Vicki's requests seemed harmless on the surface, they actually represented an invitation to a tug-of-war to determine her mother's strength and willingness to flex her muscles. As long as Mom gave in to the child's demands, Vicki continued to pull harder on her end of the rope. Eventually, Mom yanked her end of the rope, in a sense, and ended the skirmish. Although Vicki ultimately lost the conflict, she had put up an admirable fight and had enjoyed a few moments of supremacy over her mom.

Situations similar to this one can be avoided with a little bit of advanced planning on the part of the parent. A rule in Vicki's house could be discussed and agreed on that all matters requiring parental attention be tended to prior to bedtime. There might be a period of several minutes each evening allotted to taking care of the various items of concern that had previously cropped up. Then, Mom should decline any "invitations to battle" in the form of persistent, innocent requests from Vicki by ignoring those requests.

The power of the parent can be an intimidating force to some children. Youngsters may challenge that power in blatant ways or by more subtle methods. Parents must constantly be aware of potential situations that may result in a struggle for dominance, make efforts to prevent situations that breed conflict, and calmly reject invitations to fuss, fight, and bicker with a youngster. A sense of responsibility is thus communicated to children. They learn they are capable of relating in a mature manner to others in the home and are expected to resolve differences in a rational, realistic manner. Children become valued members of the same team. Rather than pulling against one another, parents and children work cooperatively, and children see home as a place of harmony.

*Whatever your task, work heartily,*
*as serving the Lord and not men*
(COL. 3:23 RSV).

# 9

# A Plea for Unity

It was Saturday morning and by nine o'clock Joni was showing signs of boredom. The cartoon programs she had been watching were no longer captivating her attention. She had already beaten her brother in two or three games of Ping-Pong in the garage. She was itching to go outside and be with her playmates, although she knew that her best friend, Betty, usually slept late on Saturday mornings. It wouldn't hurt to ask Mom, however, if she could walk down to Betty's house to check.

"Mom, is it okay for me to go to Betty's to see if she can come outside?"

Her knowing mother replied, "Betty's family is slow to get going on Saturdays. I think it would be wise for you to wait a little while before going down there."

Joni was disappointed. She knew that Mom was probably right, but she just had to find something to do! Then a thought hit her. "Why not ask Dad if I can go to Betty's house? He hasn't said yet that I couldn't go. Of course, I won't mention my conversation with Mom. What Dad doesn't know is his own responsibility."

Joni found her father in his bedroom. "Dad, is it okay for me to go to Betty's house to see if she can come outside?"

Dad was not as knowledgeable of the neighbors' sleeping habits as Mom. "Do you think they're up?" he asked.

"I've been up two and a half hours, Dad. Most kids I know get up early on Saturday morning."

"I guess so, then. Be sure to stay outside, though. I don't want you to pester Betty's parents this early in the day."

"It worked," thought Joni as she slipped past her mother, traipsing innocently out the front door and down the street to Betty's house. "I knew I could get Dad to let me go."

How many times have you been innocently tricked or deceived by your own child? Children can be masters of finding a way to gain parental approval for their actions. Joni did not like the response her mother had given to her, so she turned to her father with the hope that he would see things differently and grant her request. If questioned later by her mother about her trip to Betty's house, Joni could handily point out the approval her father had given to her. It wasn't her fault that Mom and Dad had given her two opposite responses. She simply had chosen the better of the two, and did nothing that had not been cleared by one of them.

Mom and Dad had actually done nothing wrong in this instance. It was Joni who had misused them for her own advantage. To deal effectively with this type of problem, parents need to establish a unified approach to dealing with their children. They must agree on how to handle situations that may arise in their home, and follow a consistent procedure. You might ask how a situation such as this can be avoided. It was Joni's devious behavior, not a lack of unity on the parents' part, that resulted in the girl's skirting around her mother's directive.

It is probable that Joni had played one parent against

another before, giving the parents the need to set a standard for dealing with such behavior. They could have
decided that in situations in which their child asked for
such things as permission to visit a friend, between-meal
snacks, extra privileges, spending money, or other minor
requests, they would informally check with one another
on the matter. They might choose to do so by asking
Joni, "What did Mom/Dad say about it?" or, "It's fine
with me, if Mom/Dad says so," or by asking the other,
"Honey, do you think it's okay for Joni to go down to
Betty's house?"

The intent of this way of operating is not to convey
distrust in their daughter, for they may, and should, agree
that as their daughter's ploys decrease or end, they will
decrease their set procedure. Their unity, however, says
that in their household it is not acceptable or honest to
disregard one family member's decision in the hope of
finding another family member who will make the more
desirable decision. Children are thus taught to respect
the integrity of each parent, to be considerate of all family members, and to not condone deceit.

Unity between parents avoids the temptation for children to take advantage of disagreements and misbehave
by forcing an issue to a head (which does delight some
children).

Larry was riding his bicycle up and down the street
with two of his friends. The boys were competing with
one another to see who could make the longest skid
marks on the pavement by slamming on their brakes
while traveling at a high rate of speed. Mother and Dad
were outside working in the yard. Mother in particular
was worried that Larry might fall from his bike and injure
himself, blow out a tire, or wreck his bike. After one
especially long daredevil skid in which her son nearly
tumbled to the pavement, Mother had had enough.

"Larry," she yelled. "Come here!"

Larry triumphantly pedaled to the curb beside his

mother and braked. "How'd you like that? That's the longest one yet!"

"That's true, Son," she said. "But I'm afraid you might hurt yourself, or at least tear up your bike. Would you not ride it in such a rough manner?"

"Oh, Mother. I won't get hurt. I'm being careful."

"Larry, I don't think you're being very safe. I'm telling you to stop riding your bike that way!"

Larry rode off—safely—and looked with envy as his two friends continued their competition. After a few minutes, he noticed that his mother had gone inside, leaving Dad in the yard alone. He rode up to his dad and confided in him. "Hey, Dad, Steve and Jimmy are still skidding on their bikes and they're not having wrecks. Can I play with them? I'll be careful."

Dad knew his son had been having fun when his play was halted. Feeling sorry for the boy, he told him, "I guess so, but don't let Mother see you. And if you blow out a tire, you'll have to pay for it."

"Don't worry, I won't," promised Larry as he sped off.

Larry had a hunch that his dad felt differently about the matter. When the timing was right, he coerced Dad into changing his mother's policy.

Suppose Mother caught Larry doing what she had told him not to do. Imagine the argument that would have ensued, not between Larry and Mother (although he would have been spoken to) but between Mother and Dad. What was the big idea of his telling Larry he could ride dangerously on his bike when she had instructed him not to? And so on.

What were the results of this incident? For one thing, Larry was encouraged to disobey his mother. He was indirectly told that what she said was unimportant. Second, he got the idea that behavioral limits are made to be expanded. If Larry was a smart boy (in fact, even if he was not so smart), he would learn to always look for a way around the rules. There's bound to be a loophole. If he couldn't readily find it, perhaps Mother or Dad would open it for him.

How should parents deal with instances involving disagreements between them? It is of the utmost importance that the matter be dealt with away from the presence of the children. To discuss disagreements on policy matters in front of children only increases their knowledge of the weaknesses that exist and provides them with information on how to manipulate their parents the next time similar circumstances occur. A long-term consequence is that it contributes to a damaging atmosphere of confusion in the house.

In deciding and agreeing on how specific matters concerning their children are to be dealt with, compromises will certainly be required of both parents. For example, Mr. Thompson felt very strongly that his children should eat only a limited amount of sweets, while his wife was not as concerned about what the kids ate just as long as their daily nutritional needs were met. In a conference, Mr. and Mrs. Thompson agreed that, while sweets were generally not good for their children's health, they would not totally deprive their youngsters of all such treats. Their children would have no more than one "sweet" each day, such as candy, cakes, cookies. They would substitute fruits when possible for between-meal snacks. The plan was agreeable to both of them; each had compromised. From that point forward, reference to their decision could be made whenever the problem of their children and sweets arose.

Unity between parents translates to security for the child. It is healthy for the child to realize that his parents work cooperatively. From them he learns the value of mutual trust and respect. He is better able to view the family as a unit and not as individuals in competition with one another.

*The highest and most profitable
reading is the true knowledge and
consideration of ourselves.*
THOMAS À KEMPIS

# 10

# How Do You Feel
# About Yourself?

Perhaps the most important task of parents is to rear children who will have healthy concepts of themselves. Children's self-concepts are directly related to what their parents believe their children to be. Children whose parents rear them as troublesome and hard to live with will often come to see themselves as being of little value, and their lifestyles will reflect that. Conversely, youngsters whose parents tell them in word and action that they are worthy of love and pleasant to be around will more likely grow to be lovable and pleasant.

It is vital to understand that the parents' own self-images also play a very important role in the development of their children's self-esteem. That is, what parents feel about themselves is passed along to their children.

Denny was a twenty-year-old college student who sought help in the way of professional counseling. Although he was from a family that was relatively successful by the world's standards, he had chronic loneliness and even anger that he could not fully understand. When asked to describe his own concept of himself, Denny depicted himself as one who was not satisfied with his achievements, even though he was a good student and had been a better-than-average high school athlete. He did not like the way he was, thought that others did not like his ideas, and felt that others weren't really interested in listening to his problems. On top of all that, he was sure he had disappointed others, namely his parents, and that despite his various achievements he had not accomplished any deeds worthy of praise.

Denny was initially reluctant to talk about his family, but did express the feeling that his parents, especially his father, had expected too much of him. In time, this young man painted a picture of his father that gave a good indication of the home atmosphere in which he was raised. Denny's dad, Mr. Riley, was a man who had to work hard all of his life to make any advancement or improvement. He had come from a family that was poor and had lost what little they had during the Great Depression. As he reached adulthood, Denny's father landed a sales position with a small business firm. In time, the firm grew and prospered, and Mr. Riley benefited from this growth in the way of promotions and salary increases. In spite of his business success, however, he was an unhappy man who was never satisfied with his position in life. Not surprisingly, Denny's dad had the same general personality characteristics that his son had acquired. He did not like the way he was, failed to acknowledge his accomplishments, and tended to be a despairing man. It was Mr. Riley's aim to prevent his son from living the same life he had lived. For this reason, he set high standards for Denny to follow and lofty goals for him to reach. He was not an affectionate father nor appreciative of his son's accomplishments.

An understanding of Mr. Riley's self-concept provided an insight into Denny's negative feelings about himself.

To the child whose world was largely his parents' world (as is the world of most children), low self-esteem was the norm and an insidious character trait he absorbed.

The flip side of Denny's burden was that his father had convinced himself that if his son became a success in life, his own self-image would be enhanced. He had placed all his marbles on Denny! Too often parents look to their children to feel good about themselves. Or they see their children as reflections of themselves: if their children turn out to be good, then they are good; if their children are bad, then they are bad.

Ideally, parents' self-images should be so stable that they do not depend on their children's personalities or achievements for their identity or affirmation of their own worth. On the other hand, parents who fail to accept their own incompetencies and weaknesses will likely fail to accept those weaknesses in their children, thus making them feel incomplete, not as good as they should be, flawed. Still, it is interesting to observe that virtually all parents who believe that their children are inferior to other children, not worth loving, not trustworthy, have very similar feelings about themselves. Parents' low self-images can become stumbling blocks for putting into action all the other good parenting skills they may have.

Conversely, parents who see their children as worthy of respect, capable of growth and maturation, also view themselves in that manner. Parents with healthy self-concepts are not haughty with elevated ideas of themselves, but see themselves realistically. They know and accept their limitations, have healthy love for themselves, and are willing and able to give love to others.

Likely, a great number of readers, possibly the majority, are at this point thinking that since they have less-than-perfect self-concepts, what are they to do?

It's true that most adults and many children struggle with some degree of low self-esteem. That does not mean, however, that the reader should despair of being a good parent.

Recognizing in yourself the traits that are tied to your concept of yourself is a big first step. Listen to yourself. How do you respond to life's big and little situations? Are you irritated, defeated, defensive, hopeless, self-deprecating, sorry for yourself, critical, fretful? These things not only give you away, so to speak, but set the tone of your family's home life and general outlook.

Controlling your outward responses to life is the second step, but easier said than done. Granted, you cannot at the snap of a finger completely reverse your layers of experience and years of development that have made your perception of yourself what it is. However, observing your behavior with an eye to changing what must be changed for the good of your children is both possible and profitable. Catch yourself and hold your tongue when that critical comment wants to surface. Wage a private campaign to say only encouraging instead of discouraging things to your children. Make an effort—and it may be a herculean effort—to see only the admirable things in your children and ignore their imperfections. You will be surprised how after a while their desirable behaviors will increase and their undesirable behaviors will decline.

Finally, love yourself. Really. Believe that you are worthy of your own love. God loves you, and he wants you to love whom he loves—everyone, including yourself. But your own dad didn't love you? Forget him. Likely, he did not love himself either, but for the sake of your children, forget him. For in loving yourself you will be freer to love your children for what they really are with all their talents or limitations, their charms or quirks, and not for their potential for enhancing yourself.

For some, learning self-love may begin as simply as finding one small thing to accomplish and to be proud of. For others it may begin as seriously as seeking psychotherapy. But remember, in making a healthy home atmosphere for your children, you, parent, are the important one—to yourself and to them. And you deserve the rewards and satisfactions that can come from parenting.

*Train up a child in the way he
should go, and when he is old,
he will not depart from it*
(PROV. 22:6 RSV).

# 11

# Where's the Ten O'clock Train?

Have you ever been in a train depot, bus station, or airport waiting for a late train, bus, or airplane? Doubtless, every individual who has traveled even a minimal amount has experienced this modern-day problem. Try to remember some of the feelings you had at that time. You were probably frustrated that your plans were being delayed. You may have had tension all over your body because it was important that you arrive at your destination on time. You also may have been angry at the management or transportation personnel because they were the ones causing you to be late. If the wait became long, you probably got restless and even a little bit irritable with the one sitting beside you. No one likes to be in a situation that does not go as planned.

The McFarlen home was one of seeming bedlam. Mr. McFarlen often worked long and irregular hours, leaving his wife and two children at home to fend for themselves. It seemed that the task of getting the children up in the mornings and off to school became more complicated each day. It was rare for Mom or Dad to rise early in the morning, for they had a habit of keeping late night hours. Although Mrs. McFarlen always had good intentions of getting up early to fix a good breakfast for her family while also allowing time to dress and groom the children, her plans usually were not carried out. The normal morning pattern consisted of Mrs. McFarlen dragging herself out of bed late, rushing into the kids' rooms to awaken them, helping them to get dressed, hurriedly fixing them a bowl of cereal, and seeing them off (late) to school.

The rest of the day was usually not an improvement over the morning. It seemed that there was always some place to take the children in the afternoon or early evening. Suppertime came whenever Mom had time to throw some food together and put it on the table. Nighttime activities varied. Some evenings the family had to be at church or social functions. Some evenings were spent visiting friends and relatives. Only occasionally would the family spend an evening together at home. Bedtime came when everyone was too tired to go any longer.

Living in a home that has no routine is analogous to going to the airport daily without knowing what time your airplane leaves. It is confusing and does little to promote an atmosphere of calm. It also does little to provide children the security that comes from knowing their world is a predictable place.

There are several harmful outgrowths for children in a home that has an irregular schedule of activities. Some parents may maintain that children who live in households that are always on the go with very busy schedules of activities will grow up with a strong sense of independence and the ability to take care of themselves. However, the opposite is true.

Children, especially young children, who are exposed to irregular routines fail to develop a sense of responsibility to themselves, their family members, and others.

They learn that the time to get up in the morning is when their eyes open, school begins when they arrive, mealtime is whenever food is placed in their mouths, and the time for swimming lessons is whenever they are ready to go. Children learn that the ones most likely to meet their needs for food, rest, and meaningful interaction with others (their parents), cannot be depended on. Eventually they reach the point where they look out only for themselves and fail to see the needs of others.

Psychologists tell us that the most basic needs of life must be met before more "noble" needs, such as the need to be productive, or the need to know and understand can effectively be addressed. Children in disorganized home environments must so frequently tend to gratifying their basic needs they cannot focus on those higher issues of life. They have no time to ponder the size of the universe as they look at the night sky, cultivate an interest in an elderly grandparent who wants to be part of their grandchildren's world, or wonder who God is and what he does. Their time and energy go to finding clean clothes to wear, making it to the next soccer practice, and deciding whether to order chocolate or vanilla milk shakes with their hamburgers and french fries.

A second outcome of the disorganized home is that the parent has difficulty finding time to spend constructively with the children, giving the children too much leeway and opportunity for misbehavior. At best, the harried parent can only "put out fires," but fails to develop a systematic and effective approach to "fire prevention."

Mrs. Banks was exasperated! It was one of those mornings. She had intended to have an orderly Saturday morning, but it hadn't worked out that way. Scott had a Scout meeting at ten o'clock, and Amy was invited to a birthday party a half hour later. Before Mrs. Banks knew it, the clock read nine forty-five.

"Scott!" she shouted down the hallway. "Are you dressed yet? It's time to go!"

"Coming, Mom," replied Scott, even though he was not.

"Amy, that goes for you, too! We'll just go to your party after we take Scott. Do you have that present ready for me to wrap?" She walked into Amy's room to find her daughter searching high and low for her friend's gift.

"I can't find it, Mom," wailed an exasperated Amy.

"Oh, Amy. I told you to get that gift to me last night so I could wrap it, and here it is time to go and you can't even find it!"

"But Mom . . ."

"I don't want to hear your excuses," came the stern reply. "You know that you were supposed to keep up with that gift. Don't blame me if it's lost. You'll just have to go to the party without one."

At that point, Scott stuck his head in Amy's room. "Mom, I can't find any clean socks or underwear."

"You can wear some of mine," giggled Amy.

"You'd better wrap them for a birthday present," came Scott's retort.

"We don't need these smart remarks. Both of you get ready right now, or we're not going anywhere today! Scott, there's some clean clothes in the laundry room." Mrs. Banks walked out of Amy's room frustrated that the morning had become so hectic—again.

"Mom, here's that present. Can you wrap it now?" called Amy from her closet. Mom quickly got out the paper and ribbon and wrapped the gift. As she did so, Scott managed to find his clothes and put them on. At ten minutes past ten o'clock, the three of them hurriedly drove off.

Whew! There are times in every family that the schedule is thrown out the window and it's "every man for himself." But a consistent lifestyle of bedlam does little to enhance the quality of family life.

The communication among the family members depicted above leaves a great deal to be desired. The only communication Mrs. Banks had with either of her children was fussing at them, ordering them to behave in a certain manner, or expressing her displeasure with them. There was no time for a more pleasant exchange between Mrs. Banks and her children, or between the siblings.

With minimal effort on the parents' part to avoid a last-minute rush, a more pleasant atmosphere can be established in the home. We have also mentioned that children benefit from such an atmosphere by knowing what is expected of them and are thereby provided a basis for predictability and security. And a third result of a regular household schedule is that it gives both parents and children points of reference by which to operate. There is a time and place for all major daily activities.

Dad had been home since late afternoon, as was his custom. Prior to the family's six o'clock dinnertime, he was outside taking care of a few small jobs. During this time his daughter was playing in the yard next door with a playmate. At five forty-five Dad called to his daughter. "Rachael, it's time to come in. We need to wash up before dinner."

"Daddy, can I stay out until Rhonda has to go in?"

"No, Rachael. It's fifteen until six. You know Mother will have dinner ready in a few minutes."

Rachael bade her friend good-by and promised to see her the following day. As she and her father walked into the house, she told him, "I didn't realize it was so late."

In this instance, the routine of eating dinner at six o'clock served the purpose of reminding Dad and Rachael of the time they were to come in for the evening meal. When Dad went out to complete some odd jobs, he knew how much time he could spend and gauged his work accordingly. In the same way, though Rachael was not ready to give up her play, the reminder from her father that it was almost dinnertime was sufficient notice for her to come into the house. She knew that Mother would not hold up supper simply because she wanted to play outside a while longer. Mother had known when to begin preparing dinner.

The presence of a regular schedule at Rachael's house prevented the problem of confusion among family members. It set limits within which they all knew what was expected of them. There was no need to spend the family's energy fussing with one another, coercing each other to stop one activity so that another could take place, or grumbling because nothing was ever done at the same time two days in a row. The atmosphere was pleasant, leaving time and energy for more worthwhile activities of individual and family growth.

Schedules take effort and are therefore easily abandoned, but in a household with a growing family they are worth it.

*The religion of a child depends on
what his mother and father are and
not on what they say.*
H. F. AMIEL

# 12

# The Heavier Side of Life

Just recently I was talking with the mother of a four-teen-year-old girl. Our conversation dealt with the importance of the atmosphere in the home and its influence on her daughter's behavior. After we had talked for a while, she said, "You know, it's awesome to think that the atmosphere I create at home has so much influence on my child. I can see that many of the choices she makes can be directly attributed to it."

Throughout this section we've explored the way a child's behavior is changed by the presence or absence of warmth, respect, trust, and by other factors in the home atmosphere. To conclude this section, I feel it necessary to discuss one other important element of the home environment: the spiritual atmosphere.

I very seldom talk to parents who are not concerned for the spiritual development of their children. What individuals decide to believe about the nature of God is the most important decision they will make in their entire lifetimes. Yet, many parents skirt this issue and fail to provide the proper atmosphere for spiritual growth. We're not reluctant to help our children decide whom to date or marry, or what job or vocational field to enter. But to create an atmosphere for spiritual growth? That side of life is too heavy!

Mr. and Mrs. Richards had three small children. Both parents had gone to church on a regular basis when they were young. In fact, they considered themselves to be Christian people. They believed in God and said grace at the dinner table on occasion. They tried to follow the Golden Rule and could be described as good, moral people.

During the years of their marriage the Richards had not developed a habit of attending church on a regular basis. They attended a local church once in a while, mostly on special occasions. Because their children were nearing school age, the Richards decided it was time for them to begin a regular routine of church attendance. Their thinking was that they wanted someone to teach their children about God. They reasoned that by taking the kids to church they could learn about basic spiritual truths and would then be well-equipped to make important decisions about their own spiritual health.

Sounds like a pretty good scheme, doesn't it? Many parents use this reasoning as a basis for their own church attendance. There was one major flaw in the Richards' plan, however. They failed to include themselves in their design! They assumed that the Sunday school teachers and ministers could be given total responsibility for developing the spiritual side of their children's lives. After all, those people were specially trained in such matters.

Children look to their parents for guidance on important issues and not-so-important issues. We cannot expect our church leaders to have a maximum effect on our children unless we, too, become a part of their spiritual education. Rather than extend the message to our family that "I am concerned for your spiritual well-being and I hope someone will help you find the answers you are looking for," we should enter the search with them. One of the most important results of having a home atmosphere that contains the elements that have been discussed in earlier chapters is that children will identify with their parents. When children feel loved, respected, trusted, and encouraged, a sense of closeness with their parents will develop. The statements that Mother and Dad make and the beliefs they hold will be valued.

It is the parent who is in the strongest position to develop the spiritual strength of the child. Children who know from their parents what it means to be loved with no strings attached are in a better position to understand and know in a personal way the unconditional love of God. It is parents who can best teach spiritual truths and demonstrate that life has real meaning and purpose.

Mr. Holt and his six-year-old daughter Lisa were on an outing one weekday evening. Because his daughter loved hamburgers, Mr. Holt decided to treat her to a meal at a fast-food hamburger restaurant. The father and daughter went inside, purchased their food, and seated themselves at a table.

As they were finishing their meal, Mr. Holt recognized a man sitting by himself several tables away. He had seen the man before through his business, but knew little about him. The man was in his fifties, had never married, and lived by himself. As Mr. Holt and Lisa prepared to leave, the father explained to his daughter, "I see a man I'd like to speak to before we walk out."

Approaching the man who appeared listless and had a lonely look on his face, Mr. Holt reached out to shake hands.

"Hello. I'm Ray Holt. I recognize you as a customer in my business and thought I'd introduce myself on our way out." A friendly, informal conversation ensued as the two men got to know one another. Lisa was introduced to him and answered several friendly questions that he asked her. As Mr. Holt and Lisa parted from their new friend, his countenance had changed. He thanked the two for introducing themselves to him, and said he hoped to see them again.

When Lisa and her dad got into their car, the youngster asked, "Daddy, why did we stop and talk to that man when we didn't even know him?"

"Well, Lisa," explained her father, "I recognized him as someone I had seen at my work before. He looked like he was lonely, and I thought it might cheer him up for us to chat with him for a few minutes."

"I think we did."

"You thought he looked happier? I thought so, too."

Lisa had been taught a lesson about unconditional love and acceptance of others that could not have been so graphically taught in a church. She had learned in Sunday school that God expects us to love one another. She had been told the Bible story of how the Good Samaritan had helped a stranger in need. It was through the action of her father, however, that she saw these spiritual truths come alive. Because Mr. Holt possessed an understanding of the concept of Christian love, he was capable of teaching his daughter.

A home atmosphere that encourages spiritual growth includes several important elements. Parents must share their own spiritual experiences with their children. Children need to know what their parents' concerns are. For example, if the parents pray for specific concerns, the children should be included in conversations about those concerns when it is appropriate.

Time should be taken on a regular basis to discuss the meaning of common religious teachings. It is irresponsible to assume that children will figure out these things on their own. As Mr. Holt did for his daughter, parents should take every opportunity to provide examples of Christian living. By doing so, parents give meaning to the values they and the church teach; the children more clearly understand those teachings and see their importance.

One common mistake is to misuse the concepts of religion and religious activity with children. Possibly the most frequent misuse is the parent making religion the basis or explanation for the laying down of strict rules and regulations. Instead of allowing religion to become the basis for a personal relationship with God, it becomes a tiresome list of dos and don'ts.

Joan was a single, twenty-five-year-old woman. She had a meaningless job with nothing much to look forward to each day. Deep inside Joan harbored a great deal of anger and resentment. Through her work with a counselor she was finally beginning to understand her emotions.

Joan grew up in a home that placed a strong emphasis on religious training. She felt the need for education of this sort, but somehow her parents had gotten away from emphasizing spiritual principles and focused almost solely on religious rules. No reasons were ever given for these rules; she simply had to follow them or God would become angry with her.

When she was caught in a lie, she was reminded of how upset God was with her. At times when she was lazy, she was referred to as "one of the devil's workers." When she argued with her siblings, she was told that her behavior was not Christian. In short, Joan had grown up being beaten with a religious club.

Few children will reach the high standards of a parent who uses religious concepts as a weapon and as a way to control children. Certainly our religious beliefs should influence the way we handle our children, but in a positive way. Rather than emphasize the punishment that God may inflict on them or dwell solely on the authority of God, it is more constructive to guide children to search for abstract truths and the applications of those spiritual teachings.

A child may be taught that his sister is not to be hit

because she has value as a person, instead of because God might get angry with him for his action. Rather than explain that God smiles only when children do their homework, a child can be taught that we should strive to be all that we can be in the same way that Jesus did, or that we all have gifts to develop as Paul taught.

Many children grow up with a sour taste for religion as Joan did. God is depicted as being not much fun to be around. Children may be continually reminded of their own inferiority or inherent sinfulness. After all, God stays mad at them most of the time. Finally, religion becomes something children learn to avoid, and they completely miss the fullness of the spiritual side of life.

Perhaps one of the most common ways parents avoid creating an atmosphere for spiritual growth is to allow their children to choose from among the many religions which one they will follow. Have you known parents who say they don't want to interfere with their children's religious decisions? Yet, in reality that is impossible.

Our entire lives are statements of our beliefs about spiritual matters. Through our own behavior we cannot help but strongly influence our children's decisions about their relationships with God. In households in which parents have no commitment to God or a church, children are likely to learn that such commitment is unnecessary. Their parents will have influenced them in that decision.

To carry this thought a step further, it is also true that the commitment a parent has toward other family members will influence the child's religious commitment. How? It is far easier for a son or a daughter to understand the concept of a loving, heavenly Father in a home in which Mom and Dad show their love and concern to one another, to their children, and even to unrelated people outside their home. Again, parents who fail to show such commitment to others have taught their children a spiritual lesson, for relationships with people and with God constitute life's dimension of spiritual love.

The desire to know and understand is a need all individuals have, children included. Children exhibit this desire to know and understand when they ask "why" questions. The incessant curiosity of a small child demonstrates this need. The adolescent who searches for the meaning behind relationships with the opposite sex manifests this need. Certainly, parents do all they can to help their child answer questions of this kind.

A part of this need for understanding is children's concept of who they are and why they are as they are. It is common for children to wonder where they came from, who made them, and all of the other things about themselves. Children cannot rely solely on religious workers to deal with these issues. Most children, even those who regularly attend church, spend far less time in formal religious instruction than with their own family members. Therefore, parents cannot de-emphasize the importance of this natural curiosity and their own influence on their children by the ways they satisfy that curiosity, for in one way or another they will be instrumental in their children's decisions about their relationships to God and other spiritual matters.

Children who are taught to care for others through example learn the spiritual concept of ministry. Children who are not given all they ask for learn the value of this world and are more appreciative of its creator. Children who see how to give to others do not become self-centered and are able to deal with others justly. Children who are allowed to make choices and are not persistently down-trodden learn to develop their own unique strengths and talents.

Spiritual principles are given to our child by us regardless of our intentions. Formal religious instruction, whether at church or at home, is but a part of the child's spiritual development. Even more significantly, we influence our child's religious choice through the models we provide through our own behaviors and beliefs. For Christian parents, this ultimately is what the home atmosphere is all about.

# PART 2

# Behavior
# Management
# Techniques

*The first duty to children is to make
them happy. If you have not made
them so, you have wronged them.*
C. BUXTON

# 13

## I'd Like My Paycheck, Please

Imagine what the unemployment rate in our country would be if people were expected to perform a job with the understanding that the work would not be rewarded in the form of a weekly or monthly paycheck. The jobless rate would likely approach 100 percent! No one wants to put forth hours of effort only to end up with nothing to show for it. The unemployment rate would probably not be a great deal lower if employees knew they would be paid only ten or fifteen dollars once each three or four months, depending on the boss's whims. That small amount, too, would hardly be worth the effort required to perform forty hours of work per week.

The above example may seem to be extreme and rather ridiculous. Of course employers must pay employees if they expect assigned jobs to be completed. Yet, many parents apply this principle of "all work and no pay" to the behavior of their children. The job description for being a child is generally set by the parent in the form of expectations the parent has for the child. For example, a parent may expect that while living at home, the son or daughter will fulfill such expectations as displaying proper manners at home and in public places, contributing to the cleanliness of the house, attending school regularly, and so forth. Under each general heading, there would be an endless number of specific applications and examples of acceptable and unacceptable behaviors. Why, an entire volume could be written to completely cover the job description of any given child!

We often go to an extreme to inform our children of the way they are expected to behave, but fail to "pay" them for what they accomplish. Too many children "work" for little or no pay.

Jason had managed to keep his bedroom clean for most of the day. After the evening meal, however, he decided to dig into his toy chest and entertain himself before getting ready for bed. He found a container of building blocks and proceeded to build an elaborate structure that he called an army fort. He strategically placed toy soldiers throughout the fort as if preparing them for battle. Taking a box of dominos he then dropped "bombs" on his fort and threw "missiles" at the stronghold as he wiped out an entire army division and destroyed a strategic military post of the enemy. Just as he completed his raid, Jason's dad looked into his bedroom.

"Jason, bedtime. Get this mess cleaned up right now!"

Jason muttered that he was just about to clean up and proceeded to do so. Following this, he readied himself for bed and walked into his parents' bedroom to find his father. "Did you see that I cleaned up my room, Dad?" he asked.

"Good," was all he heard. "Let's go to bed now."

Jason went with his father and climbed into bed without saying much to him. His dad, never acknowledging that Jason's toys had been put away, bade his son good night and quietly walked out of the room.

Jason's father didn't realize that, while his son successfully carried out his assigned task of cleaning up his room, which was part of his "job description," he failed to pay the boy in the form of a compliment or positive attention. He was, in essence, asking Jason to work without pay. His nominal acknowledgment that Jason had completed his task was hardly the reward that Jason was seeking. Notice the change of events the following day.

Jason was playing outside when dad arrived home from work. The two greeted one another cheerfully and walked into the house together. As Dad went into his bedroom to change his clothes, Jason realized that he had failed to change into his play clothes as he normally did after coming home from school. He quickly took off his pants and shirt, put on his play clothes, walked into the hallway, and dropped his school clothes by the bathroom door. Jason's dad, looking from his bedroom, noticed his son's actions.

"Just a minute, Jason," he called. "You know you're not supposed to leave your clothes there." He looked askance at Jason.

"Oh, I just wanted Mom to be sure to see them so she'll wash them for me," explained Jason as he turned to walk away.

"Jason, put them into the clothes hamper like we always do. You know Mom will wash your clothes."

"Aw, Dad, I don't want to. Let someone else put those dumb ol' clothes in the hamper." Jason looked at his dad from the corner of his eye, expecting a reaction.

"Put them away now, or I'll take off my belt. You know better than to act like that." Dad held Jason's arm firmly and moved him in the direction of the dirty clothes. Realizing that he had gone as far as his dad would allow without taking more stringent measures, Jason complied with the order. As the two separated, Dad couldn't help but wonder what had gotten into his son. It wasn't like him to be oppositional like that.

An understanding of Jason's motives provides an

explanation for his behavior. He wanted to make certain his dad took notice of his behavior. The previous night he had done as his father told him to do and failed to receive an adequate reward. To avoid a repeat of the same disappointing situation, he chose to act in a way that his dad could not help but notice. What better way could this goal be accomplished than by forcing his dad to pay attention to him? He had learned the previous night (and probably many times before) that by simply conforming to the rules of the house without causing a stir he did not attract nearly as much attention as when he involved his dad in a struggle. In his own way, Jason had concluded that negative attention was preferred to no attention at all.

One of the first rules of behavior that must be applied to the management of children is that all people want to be rewarded in some way for their behavior. A reward may take any variety of shapes. The most common reward sought by children is one that costs absolutely nothing: attention! One of the basic psychological needs any child or adult has is a sense of belonging to and being loved by others. For a child this need is satisfied when he receives attention from others: he is noticed as being a person of worth.

A great deal of a child's behavior is intended to elicit a response, hopefully positive, from another person. Frequently, that person is the parent. Predictably, the child who is unable to gain positive attention from Mother or Dad (like Jason above) will resort to less acceptable means of gaining the assurance that his parents notice and therefore love him. Unfortunately for the child, his desperate appeals for attention generally invite a negative parental response, resulting in the implication that he is *not* worthy of love. To relate this concept to the analogy of the employee seeking pay from the employer, the child who seeks attention in a negative way from his parents only to be rejected is like the salesman who, because he works on a commission, *oversells* his product, which results in no sales and no pay from his employer.

What is important to one child may have no appeal whatsoever to another. At the Lewis household, Mother decided one evening to prepare asparagus for dinner, since it was one of her favorite vegetables. She knew, however, that there was a risk involved in preparing this dish. Her two boys did not like asparagus. Because it was an expensive vegetable, she did not want it to be wasted. She determined before supper that she would offer a reward to her boys for eating the vegetable—a dish of ice cream following their meal. The plan worked beautifully for Ronnie, but flopped when it came to Ricky. There was nothing more appealing to Ronnie than a dish of ice cream, so he decided to gulp down his asparagus to get the payoff. Ricky, however, did not think highly of his mother's plan and failed to follow through with eating the asparagus. In his mind the plan called for too much work on his part (eating an atrocious vegetable) for too little pay.

Many parents ask, "Is it necessary that I always tell my child in advance what the reward will be for a certain behavior?" The answer is No. In the same way that an employee enjoys a surprise bonus at Christmastime, the child enjoys unexpected reinforcement for appropriate behavior.

Mr. Brooks had a day's work ahead of him one Saturday and asked his two sons to help him. The first task on his list was to clean the gutters. Following that was raking leaves and gathering them into bags. Next, the lawn needed mowing and fertilizing. After a full day of work, both boys and their dad were exhausted, but pleased to see their chores completed. That evening at the dinner table, Dad recognized the boys in the presence of the rest of the family.

"John and Jody really helped me a great deal doing yard work today. I don't believe I would have finished all that needed to be done without their help."

He then reached into his pocket and pulled out some money and gave it to the boys, who were obviously delighted. It made the hard day's work all worthwhile. It also increased Dad's effectiveness as a reinforcing agent.

Mr. Brooks may have felt it was not necessary to reward his sons in the form of paying them for work they had performed around the house. It is quite possible that in the Brooks household everyone was expected to help out with all of the duties. Yet, in this instance he chose to reward John and Jody for their efforts. By doing so he taught his sons that their diligent work efforts were noticed and appreciated. The boys also learned that the successful completion of odd jobs around the house did not have to be drudgery. It could pay them dividends. An important point to make in this example is that the money the boys received was only *one* of the rewards. Their father's acknowledgment of their accomplishments was also a powerful reinforcer. His attention to their deeds in the presence of others did a great deal to enhance their own sense of worthiness. It is likely that they will want to continue to behave responsibly, because an acknowledgment from their dad is meaningful and satisfying to them.

*Love is not happy with evil,*
*but is happy with the truth*
(1 COR. 13:6 GNB).

# 14

## Catch 'em Being Good

Mr. Jensen had agreed with his wife to talk to a psychologist about their daughter, Jan. It seemed that he and Mrs. Jensen were constantly having to scold her for her misbehavior. She never did what she was supposed to do, but always seemed to do the opposite of what her parents asked. Mr. and Mrs. Jensen could not figure out how to "train" their daughter to act in a more acceptable way. Together with the psychologist they discussed methods of using sound behavior management techniques. Mrs. Jensen was willing to apply these methods to her own way of responding to Jan, but Mr. Jensen was skeptical. "Dr. Watson, I don't see how it will work. We always punish the girl when she does wrong, but it never works over a long period of time."

Dr. Watson encouraged Mr. Jensen to complete one assignment during the next week. He gave the father a piece of paper and asked him to make one mark for each time he rewarded Jan for an appropriate behavior or reinforced a positive act on her part. Mr. Jensen agreed to the task, but expressed doubt as to the eventual outcome.

89

The following week, Mr. and Mrs. Jensen kept their appointment with the psychologist. As they walked into his office, Mr. Jensen tossed his paper on Dr. Watson's desk and proclaimed, "See, it's blank. That girl didn't do one thing for me to reinforce this entire week. I knew it wouldn't work!"

"That's really something, that *everything* she did last week was negative. Do you mean she didn't do even one good thing all week?" asked Dr. Watson.

"Not one," replied the adamant father.

"Tell me, then. What are some of the things she does that are bad? Just give me one small example," requested Dr. Watson.

"Well," thought Mr. Jensen, "every day when I drive home from work, Jan's bicycle is lying in the driveway, and I've told her a hundred times to keep her bike out of the driveway so I can park my car there."

"*Every* day the bicycle is in the driveway?" asked the psychologist.

"Well, almost every day."

"Was there any day this past week that Jan did *not* leave her bike in the driveway?"

"Probably a couple," answered the father.

"I'm interested in your response to her when you came home to find that Jan had left her bicycle somewhere besides the middle of the driveway."

"What do you mean?" asked the father, who was now more subdued and interested in the psychologist's line of thinking.

"Did you say anything complimentary to Jan for doing something that could be considered appropriate behavior, such as leaving her bike elsewhere?" Dr. Watson continued.

"I never thought of that. I'm usually relieved when I drive home to find the driveway available for my car," responded Mr. Jensen.

Mr. Jensen had missed a golden opportunity to compliment Jan for doing something right! The only time he looked for Jan (at least as far as the bicycle incident was concerned) was when she had done something wrong. He had failed to see the importance of complimenting—rewarding—her for doing something right, and that the reward would encourage her to repeat doing it right. An encouraging response in this instance might be, "Jan, I noticed that you left your bike somewhere other than in the driveway. That made it easy for me to park my car there. I'm glad you did that for me," or a simple "Thanks, Jan, for leaving your bike in the yard rather than in the driveway."

Children prefer receiving rewards to punishment—everyone knows that. Yet a common practice parents use in dealing with their children's behavior is punishing them when they are bad and ignoring them when they are good. People generally assume that children do not need attention when they are behaving correctly; that is the way they are supposed to behave. Nothing could be further from the truth! Parents should make concerted efforts to find opportunities to recognize, acknowledge, compliment, reward good behavior and therefore re-inforce it. Many parents, like Mr. Jensen, may have to look pretty hard to find a behavior to reward, but no child does *everything* completely wrong. Every child does some things well and should be recognized for the effort.

Have you ever been with a group of relatives who have in the midst of them a toddling, eighteen-month-old child who is just beginning to perform for others? The scene has been depicted over and over all across the globe. The child has the attention of everyone in the room. Once the toddler gets over initial shyness (some have no inhibitions at all), the little tyke may decide to dance or demonstrate one of his or her tricks. Do you remember the response the youngster received? Why, it was one of great reinforcement! All the adults marveled at the toddler's skills and provided the child with more attention than he or she could possibly absorb. The end result? The little actor continued to perform and put on quite a show for the captive audience.

While I am not advocating that parents and other relatives continually encourage a child to "show off," there is a valuable point to this example. When a child receives attention, praise—positive reinforcement—for a specific behavior, the natural inclination for that child is to repeat that behavior or one similar to it in the hope of receiving additional reinforcement. Children will *work* for the positive attention of others.

Five-year-old Christopher and his friend Grady were playing in the sand pile in Christopher's backyard. Christopher's mother was usually somewhat reluctant to allow the two boys to play together, because they frequently were loud and boisterous and difficult to manage. As Mother sat nearby in a lawn chair, she noticed that while they were busily playing they were more quiet than usual. The boys had dug tunnels in the sand and were driving small cars and trucks through their sand pile freeway. Mother went to the sand pile and crouched down beside the boys.

"Looks like you're building a freeway," observed Mother.

"And tunnels, too," added Christopher, obviously enjoying himself.

"Watch how my truck goes through the tunnel," said Grady.

"You know, boys, it's really been pleasant for me to sit out here with you. I've enjoyed reading my magazine while you have played together so nicely. Things are going well this afternoon."

Neither of the boys looked up, but both got the message. Mother stepped back to her lawn chair, and the boys continued their play. In a few minutes, Christopher looked at his friend and told him, "We're playing nice together."

"Yeah," acknowledged his playmate.

With a minimal amount of effort and time, Christopher's mother had taken the opportunity to reinforce the boys' appropriate behavior. A less discerning parent may have merely looked up at the boys and smiled approvingly to herself. But that would have meant nothing to the boys.

For a reinforcer to be effective, it is not necessary that an elaborate system be followed. As in the case of Christopher and Grady, a compliment may be casually given and yet have a very positive effect, with the result being an increased incidence of the behavior that was complimented or rewarded. The two boys, while not readily acknowledging the compliment from Christopher's mother, were nevertheless motivated to continue to behave appropriately. Certainly, the reinforcer would not cause a decrease in their cooperative play—it had meant a good something to them! They had been subtly informed that the effect of their behavior was pleasant. Mother enjoyed their presence.

Although few adults actually follow this rule of thumb, it is important that children have at least twice as much positive (rewarding, happy) interaction with their parents as negative (punitive, unhappy). Taking a moment to comment on the appropriate behavior of a child is no burden to a parent and will result in much less time spent correcting misbehavior or feuding and arguing with an unhappy youngster.

An obvious question regarding the use of reinforcement is, How much is enough? Do I need to compliment every instance in which my children act as they should? Is there a schedule I should follow in reinforcing my child's good behavior?

As will be further explained in the next chapter, it is necessary to reinforce a desired behavior more frequently in the initial stages of training than in the later stages. Once an acceptable behavior has been targeted by the parent it will be necessary to frequently reinforce that behavior in a way the child will come to associate positive thoughts with the behavior.

A caution is in order, however. A child who anticipates a reward following *every* instance of the desired behavior will become dependent on that reward and will quickly stop the behavior, or at least decrease the performance of it, very rapidly when the reward is not always forthcoming.

Let's go back to the example of Mr. Jensen and his daughter's bicycle. Should he become enthusiastic each time his daughter parked her bike somewhere other than the driveway and provide Jan a great deal of attention and encouragement, it is quite possible that she would become dependent on his assurance and quickly go back to her old habit once he failed to reward her. Once she demonstrated the desired behavior several days in a row, it would be wise for Mr. Jensen to decrease the number of reinforcers he provided her. He might pay special attention to her every second time that she left the driveway vacant and then every third or fourth time. Eventually, it would be necessary to compliment her only occasionally as a reminder that her appropriate behavior was recognized and appreciated. Jan would become less dependent on a reward for her behavior and regard parking her bike away from the driveway as being routine. Finally, her reward would be her own satisfaction in doing things right. Her good behavior would be completely reinforced.

*No great thing is created*
*suddenly. . . . If you tell me you*
*desire a fig, I answer you that there*
*must be time. Let it first blossom,*
*then bare fruit, then ripen.*
EPICTETUS

# 15

# You Can't Score a Touchdown on Every Play

Any football coach would drool at the prospect of fielding a team that was able to score a touchdown every time it touched the football. Actually, even a coach would have to admit, however, that would make for a boring game. The excitement of scoring would be lost in a game in which a team tallied fifty or sixty touchdowns. What makes the game is the series of plays to achieve a touchdown. Every play that is run contributes to the end result—the score—and together with other plays forms a successful drive toward the end zone.

Often parents expect to change children's undesirable behavior virtually overnight, as if they were football coaches expecting to score on every play. Like the drive for a touchdown, the task of converting a child's behavior to a more desirable form requires a series of acts that will eventually result in a "score."

Many a student of human behavior has been taught the concept of shaping behavior by first training a rat to perform a specific task (call it a trick if you like). The typical setting includes a small plexiglass box that is empty except for a short lever, or bar, that is attached to one of the walls and connected to a small receptacle located nearby. The rat (most labs use the white rat, which is cuter and not nearly as repulsive as the "street rat") is placed inside the box and allowed to roam about it at will.

The student is then told to provide the rat with a morsel of rat food any time the animal approaches the bar. Initially, close approximations to the desired behavior (pressing the bar) are reinforced, but eventually the rat is required to press the bar on his own before he gets his goodie. As the student discovers, by rewarding the little fellow for performing his trick, the incidence of the rat's bar pressing increases. He has come to associate good things (rat food) with the previously neutral act (pressing a silly little bar). Psychologists call this behavior modification.

A great deal of children's behavior is learned in the same way that the rat learns its task. Children find through trial and error of everyday living that when they behave in a certain manner they get a specific reward. A behavior that previously had been neutral becomes associated with something positive and evolves into a common occurrence.

Four-year-old Jeffrey had been told by his mother and dad that the polite thing to do when someone gave him any item or was kind to him was to respond with the words *thank you*. While these words by themselves had little value, Jeffrey used them in situations that seemed to be appropriate. In time he found that these words were usually met with a friendly "You're welcome" or a smile or a compliment on his good manners. Many adults even commented that his use of these two words caused him to seem very big and mature. Although he did not quite understand the magic of the words, he used them more regularly because he liked what took place immediately following his utterance. In time, Jeffrey developed a habit of telling people "Thank you" whenever he was given a compliment, gift, favor, or other pleasant offering. Naturally, his parents were pleased with their son for his fine etiquette.

In this example, the same principle that applied to the rat applied to the boy. He increased the behavior that was reinforced regularly by the positive effects that followed. Not all behaviors, however, are taught as easily and simply as Jeffrey's. Some behavior is more complex.

Mrs. Hinson was determined to break her afternoon routine with her two daughters. Each day the sisters would come home from school intent on going outdoors for a time of play with their friends before suppertime. Every afternoon as the girls readied themselves for play, Mrs. Hinson reminded them that they were to tidy up their room first. The girls generally gave their room a quick cleanup and usually left it in much the same condition as they found it. Frequently, Mrs. Hinson fussed at the girls because their work had not met her standards. Because of the general failure of this method, she decided on a new approach. Rather than expect the girls to clean up the entire room, she would be satisfied if only a portion of their job was completed.

That afternoon after the girls had arrived home from school, Mrs. Hinson told them, "Before you play today, I'd like you to put your shoes in the closet. Once you've done that you may do as you like, but not until then."

"Is that all?" asked Alice, the older sister.

"Yes, that's all," replied her mother. "After you've put your shoes in the closet you're free to do as you please."

"Sure!" said Alice, with her sister Candace standing beside her nodding approval. "I think we can handle that!"

Mrs. Hinson watched with satisfaction as Alice and Candace easily completed their assignment. After they had put their shoes in the closet, they did what they wished.

The following day when the two girls arrived home

after school, their mother greeted them. "Girls, today I'd like you to put your shoes in the closet and hang up the clothes you take off. Once you have done that, you may do as you like, but not until then."

"But yesterday all we had to do was put away our shoes. Why can't we just do that again today?" protested Candace.

"You did well yesterday. Today I'm sure you can do a little more," Mrs. Hinson assured them. She knew her request was not too demanding on them and had faith that they could complete their tasks. As expected, the girls did as they were requested and were allowed to choose a free-time activity.

Each day thereafter, Mrs. Hinson added a small amount of work to the girls' assignment, but never a large amount. On most days the girls completed their duty easily, but on those few days that the task was not correctly finished, the girls were not allowed their free play until it was corrected.

Over a period of two weeks, the sisters had reached the point that to gain their free play, most of their room had been cleaned. Mrs. Hinson found, unexpectedly, that Alice and Candace often tidied their room a bit before they left for school in the morning to lessen the amount of time needed in the afternoon.

Mrs. Hinson had discovered that she was expecting too much from her daughters by initially asking them to clean their entire room. That had resulted in a daily argument with the girls for failing to complete their chore, which was frustrating and ineffective. Instead, a gradual process of earning their rewards led to their required behavior.

Unfortunately, parents can reinforce undesirable behavior also, often unwittingly. It happens when children do something—anything—to get their parents' attention or favors, and the parents give in because they are worn down by the behavior or want to squelch it quickly.

Two-year-old Rudy was not quite big enough to fill a cup with juice or to operate a water faucet when he wanted a drink. He relied on his parents to get the drink for him, and since his mother was his daytime caretaker, he was often requesting aid from her. The scene was repeated many times.

"Mama," said Rudy, "I want juice."

"Wait, Rudy. I'll get it in a minute," answered Mama, who was busy in the kitchen.

"I want it now, Mama," Rudy whined, looking to his mother, who continued her work. "I want some juice." The whining became louder, and Rudy's face became longer as he pleaded for his drink.

"Rudy, I'll get it in a minute. Can't you see that my hands are dirty? You can wait a minute longer," came the unsympathetic response.

Rudy's request was being ignored, so he began to cry louder. "Mama, I'm thirsty. I want juice! I want my juice!" He tugged at his mother's leg and continued his wailing.

Mama, quite frustrated by now, looked down at the toddler. "Oh, Rudy!" came a disgusted reply. She walked to the cupboard and reached for a cup and went to the refrigerator to get the juice container. As she poured the juice into the cup, she spoke sternly to her son, "I don't want to hear any more of that whining and crying. You knew I would get you some juice. All you had to do was ask nicely. Here!" Rudy walked away, content to have his juice.

In this instance, Mama had shaped Rudy's behavior so he learned that to have a request fulfilled by her it was necessary to whine or cry. Although his mother told him that he merely had to ask quietly for a cup of juice, his experiences taught him otherwise. He knew that as his behavior became more intolerable and his voice louder, he was more likely to gain the attention he sought and the desired favor from his mother. His crying and making a general nuisance of himself had actually been reinforced.

Both acceptable and unacceptable behaviors are usually learned gradually over a period of time. Parents who set out to correct behavior often expect sudden change in their children. It must be remembered that the undesirable behavior may be the result of a long and well-established pattern of reinforcement. It is through gradual and steady change that improvements are brought about.

*Even a child is known by his*
*actions*
(PROV. 20:11 NIV).

# 16

## The Grandmother Principle

Nothing I have ever done for that girl has ever been appreciated! I have tried to do everything I can possibly think of to encourage good behavior. I have praised her, given her money, bought things for her, let her stay up late on weekends, and she still acts terrible!"

Those words have a familiar ring to them. In the last chapter we saw how both acceptable and unacceptable behaviors of children are reinforced. We would like to believe the ideal course is to teach positive behavior through positive reinforcement. But it can be a herculean task to identify what is likely to be reinforcing to a child. There are few things that are more deflating to a parent than to hear a child say, "So who said I like that?"

One form of behavior modification is something we're all familiar with: the grandmother principle. This says you must eat your green beans before you get dessert. It demands that you put your bicycle in the garage before you watch television. It declares that you must complete your chores before going out on Saturday night.

The grandmother principle teaches us that one behavior—an activity the child enjoys—can be used to reinforce another behavior. The joy of eating dessert can be used as a reinforcer for the act of eating green beans. The fun of television watching can be employed as a reinforcer for routinely putting away a bicycle. The opportunity to be with friends reinforces the effort of completing a chore. In other words, the grandmother principle says that a behavior a child delights to do frequently may be a reward to increase behavior the child tries to avoid.

This principle is commonly used in altering children's behavior. But, because it is such a seemingly trite form of behavior modification, it is not used to its fullest extent. It can be especially useful in cases in which parents have difficulty identifying what might be reinforcing for their children.

Eight-year-old Dee suffered a severely broken leg as a result of a bad fall she took from her horse. She was hospitalized for three weeks, during which time she underwent two surgeries. Following her discharge, Dee required extensive care at home for four more weeks. Her mother was her constant companion. During the day, Mother helped Dee stay caught up with her school work, played games with her to pass the time, and listened to her talk of her plans to become involved in normal childhood activities.

As is often the case during convalescent periods, Dee developed several bad habits. Initially her family ignored them, not wanting to upset her during her recovery. Most of her annoying habits decreased as her health improved. However, she stubbornly refused to do the exercises prescribed by her physical therapist. As she gained strength, she was to get out of bed and move about on her crutches several times a day, and also to lie in bed and lift her healing leg up and down twenty-five times, three times daily. Dee's parents knew that her unwillingness to perform these exercises would result in a prolonged recovery period.

Dee's parents devised a program using rewards to encourage her to do her physical therapy. Over several days Dee's mom noted that Dee's time was spent reading books, watching television, playing board games, eating meals, all while Dee sat on her favorite couch. Family members allowed her to designate that piece of furniture as hers during her recovery. Thus, Mom concluded Dee's most frequent and therefore preferred behavior was sitting on her couch.

Putting the grandmother principle into effect, Dee's mother told her the plan was to be that before she sat on the couch each morning, afternoon, and evening, she would have to successfully complete her exercises.

The first few days Dee challenged her mother. She complied on occasion to the provision that she perform her leg exercises prior to sitting on the couch. She refused at other times and chose to sit elsewhere. But, no other chair was comfortable to her. She did not savor the thought of lying in bed—that was too boring. Her grumbling of her discomfort told Mom that the plan was working. Within a matter of a few days she was successfully accomplishing her assigned task regularly—and getting to sit on her favorite piece of furniture.

Dee's mother had shown creativity in identifying a reinforcer that had meaning, by looking beyond the obvious sources of reinforcement—watching television, reading books, and so forth—and recognized a frequent behavior that had meaning for her daughter.

One reason the grandmother principle can fail is the tendency of adults to impose their own values in defining a positive reinforcer. In Dee's case, it would have been a mistake to make television-viewing privileges contingent on the performance of her exercises. She had other activities to substitute for that behavior. Dee's mother may have cringed at the thought of not being able to read books herself, but Dee would have found a replacement for that activity. By putting personal value aside and viewing Dee's situation from her point of view, her mother found and used a meaningful positive reinforcer.

This method was also utilized quite effectively by the parents of a fourteen-year-old girl, Faye. Faye had developed a bad case of "junior high-itis." Those in regular contact with young adolescents are familiar with its symptoms: frequent silly behavior, intense interest in members of the opposite sex, a preoccupation with one's social status, and the constant worry about one's outward appearance.

In many ways Faye's parents enjoyed their daughter's phase of development. But one of its drawbacks was the problem that afflicts so many early adolescents. Faye had become disinterested in school to the point that her report card grades took a serious nose-dive.

Rather than hit the panic button, Faye's mom and dad took responsible action by developing a plan to encourage their daughter to be more dependable in her classroom duties. They took an inventory of all of Faye's activities, and found that Faye engaged regularly in one in particular: she constantly experimented with her makeup. She immensely enjoyed trying different colors of eye shadow, various shades of lipstick, and the like.

A behavior management scheme was born. Faye was told that her makeup privileges would be given on a weekly basis. Wearing makeup, a frequent behavior, would become a reward or reinforcer for her completing and turning in classroom assignments, an infrequent behavior. It worked. Because Faye's physical appearance was important to her, she worked to receive the reinforcer of experimenting with various makeup products.

Too often, parents get bogged down trying to identify reinforcers powerful enough to be used positively. Circumstances will arise in which creativity is required to develop a plan of action that effectively motivates a child. A theme that runs through this book centers around the need to look at life from the child's point of view. A complete understanding of the child allows the parent to identify the child's chosen frequent behaviors that may become reinforcers for increasing necessary but infrequent behaviors. This principle of behavior modification works. Just ask Grandmother!

*Discipline your son,*
*and he will give you peace;*
*he will bring delight to your soul*
(PROV. 29:17 NIV).

# 17

# Call on the Fire Department!

Although it would be ideal, and probably simpler, to raise children to behave well only through using positive reinforcement (rewards) for positive behavior, the darker side of life is that real children also develop negative (undesirable) behavior. For example, suppose a parent can readily see that a child throws too many temper tantrums. How do you get the child to stop? Oh, that it were possible to simply call the fire department to come put out the fire! Let's take the principle of behavior modification and see how it can help parents deal with problem behavior.

You will recall from our example in chapter 15 that a rat learns to press a bar by receiving a pellet of rat food for doing so. It's no surprise what happens when the rat no longer gets a reward for pressing the bar. Initially, he continues to press the bar, in fact even more vigorously than before. The little fellow assumes, perhaps, that the contraption is malfunctioning or that whoever controls the device failed to notice him. In time, however, he will come to realize that when he presses the bar nothing happens. The frequency of bar pressing will decrease and eventually cease altogether. It is interesting to note, however, that even long after the bar pressing behavior has been eliminated, a single reward for a casual push on the bar will quickly cause the clever rat to continue, once again, his old habit until the behavior is eliminated once again by a withholding of rewards. The rat never completely loses the capacity for his old behavior and can very quickly be retrained to perform it.

You've probably correctly guessed that I'm about to point out that this principle for eliminating behavior is also effective for children. Children, as we have seen, perform certain behaviors because of the effects that follow, particularly if they receive attention. Therefore, withholding a reinforcement of an undesirable behavior can be one effective way to stop it.

Dennis, nine years old, was being a general pest one evening. His mother and dad had invited another couple to eat dinner with them. Dennis had been a picture of politeness during the mealtime, but he had also been ignored by the adults. Oh, sure, a comment or two were directed toward him, but nothing satisfying to him.

Following dinner, the adults made their way into the living room to drink coffee and chat informally. Dennis, who was growing tired of being ignored, gathered some toys and sat in a corner of the room playing quietly. As time passed, he became more and more boisterous and began to create quite a commotion.

"Dennis," asked his mother politely, "would you please hold it down? We're trying to talk over here."

Dennis looked up at his mother and saw her smile at him. He smiled back and quietly resumed his play. After only a minute, he started laughing loudly at his imaginary play. He was having a great time!

"Dennis," came Dad's voice, "Mom has already asked you to be a little more quiet. That's not too much for us to ask of you, is it?"

"No, sir. I got carried away, I guess." He looked at his parents' guests and saw them smiling at him. It was obvious they thought he was cute. He enjoyed their brief attention. The next time, not only did he play loudly and laugh, he also sang songs. Dennis's observant father noticed his son glancing frequently over his shoulder to see that his noise was getting attention. Dad signaled to his wife and guests to ignore Dennis. While it was difficult to ignore such a racket, they did so. In response to their silence, Dennis increased his level of noise. But after several minutes he tired and once again resumed quiet play.

In this instance, Dennis sought attention from his parents and their friends, a natural behavior, but sought it in an inappropriate way. When his efforts to force the adults to notice him proved to be fruitful, he worked vigorously for continued reinforcement. Dad realized what his son was up to and arranged to withdraw any attention from Dennis as long as he was displaying this undesirable behavior. Quite naturally, the boy sought frantically to regain the reinforcement, but when he received no reward, he reduced and finally ended his behavior.

The astute reader has probably noted that Dennis's parents could have avoided their son's noisy behavior altogether had they merely given him attention for his good behavior. The point here, however, is that by completely withholding reinforcers for inappropriate behavior, that behavior will eventually disappear. The typical pattern is that following the loss of a reward the child dramatically increases the problem behavior in an all-out effort to regain the reward, then steadily reduces and finally gives up the behavior altogether.

One of the most common behaviors children use to gain attention from parents is the temper tantrum. Probably any adult who has had children would agree that there must be a secret pact among children on a world-wide basis to continue the tradition of the temper tantrum, it's that common!

Mrs. Mavis had reached her wit's end. Over the past weeks her four-year-old son, Stanley, had developed a tendency to throw a temper tantrum whenever his younger brother, Steve, age two, crossed him. One day Stanley and Steve were in their bedroom playing separately with their toys. Stanley was busily working a puzzle and had just about completed it when his little brother began to annoy him by taking out some of the pieces that had been laid in place. Stanley grabbed the puzzle pieces from Steve, which caused him to cry. Hearing the noise, Mrs. Mavis went to their room.

"What now?" she asked, looking at the brothers with disgust.

"He took my puzzle away from me!" whined Stanley.

"I wanna play, Mama," answered Steve.

Then, with little forewarning, Stanley escalated into a temper tantrum. He began to cry and shouted, "He *always* takes my things. I *never* get to work my puzzles by myself. They're *my* puzzles, and he's in my way!"

Mother tried to quiet her older son while Steve looked on. Her talk, however, did little to pacify Stanley. As he continued to cry, Mrs. Mavis realized that Steve probably had intruded on Stanley's territory. She reached into Steve's hand, took the puzzle piece, and handed it to Stanley.

"Here. Now be quiet. He wasn't trying to bother you," Mother said firmly.

With that problem solved, temporarily at least, Mrs. Mavis left the boys once again playing quietly. When she was out of earshot, Stanley sternly warned his younger brother, "Don't bother me anymore, or I'll do the same thing again."

Wow! Stanley was pretty smart. Mrs. Mavis could not understand why he had developed a penchant for throwing tantrums, but he had discovered they proved to be an effective way to manipulate her. By crying and shouting there was an increased likelihood that Mother would rule in his favor.

So what should Mrs. Mavis do? Her major objective was to stop each outburst as soon as possible. But she had failed to notice the long-term effect of her approach to this behavior problem. While she could successfully squelch a temper tantrum temporarily by giving in to Stanley's demand, she encouraged him to repeat them whenever he thought they were to his advantage. Stanley got the reward he sought, so there was no reason for him to change.

Mrs. Mavis's emphasis should be shifted from the short-term problem of solving a simple dispute between her sons to the more serious problem of Stanley's tantrum behavior as an inappropriate method of interacting with his mother. Once the outburst began, Mother should have taken Steve (and the puzzle piece in dispute) and left the room with a calmly presented message that they would return once he had finished his tantrum. With no one in his presence to give him attention, Stanley would have had the choice of continuing to throw a fit without an audience or to begin to behave in a good way that would regain attention from his mother. Since the desire for attention and thus controlling the situation on his terms was the whole purpose behind his behavior, he would most likely eventually choose the latter. Probably his noise level would increase immediately after his mother and brother left the room, but eventually his behavior would steadily decline and stop when he realized a reward was not forthcoming.

Perhaps one of the most difficult situations is when a child throws a tantrum in a public place, such as in church or a store. The child knows how to use that added pressure to get the parents' response.

The Woodleys were at a local supermarket to pick up a few items on their way to visit the children's grandparents. While they were in the store, ten-year-old Mickey saw a stuffed doll that tickled her fancy. "Oh look!" she exclaimed to her parents. "Don't you love that doll?"

"It's cute, isn't it?" agreed her father. "Put it away and let's hurry. We've got several things to get."

"Daddy," asked Mickey in her sweetest voice, "can we buy it? It isn't much."

"No, sugar, we're not here to buy dolls. Put it back, please."

Mickey's voice rose. "But Daddy, why can't I have it? You haven't bought me anything new lately." The observant daughter noticed that her parents were uncomfortable with other shoppers looking at them. Her whining escalated.

Dad, wisely not succumbing to her high-pressured tactics to manipulate him, gave his wallet to Mother so she could pay for the groceries and quietly escorted his daughter out of the store. Even though she continued to fuss and complain loudly, he remained calm and failed to reward her by attending to her unruly actions. Once they got to the car, he allowed Mickey to sit in the car and complete her tantrum while he waited outside.

Although Mickey certainly created an undesirable situation for her parents and was rewarded to some extent by the attention she gained from other shoppers, she did not receive the full reward she initially sought—compliance to her demands by her parents. Her father, who realized that he could not completely eliminate all reinforcers, did the best that could be done to eliminate as many reinforcers as possible by calmly removing her from the presence of others whose attention was stimulating to her and then allowed her to complete her behavior without the benefit of a reward.

In some cases, our best response is to make no response at all: our silence tells our children their behavior will not be reinforced. That leaves them no choice but to behave acceptably.

*If I could get to the highest place in
Athens, I would lift up my voice
and say: "What mean ye, fellow
citizens, that ye turn every stone to
scrape wealth together, and take so
little care of your children, to whom
ye must one day relinquish all?"*
SOCRATES

# 18

# Substitute, Please

An effective way of eliminating a child's inappropriate behavior is to substitute new or different behaviors. As we have already noted, children will behave so as to gain some type of reward or reinforcement, and in many instances will resort to outlandish means to gain that reward. However, a child who is rewarded for a positive behavior that is incompatible with the negative behavior will soon substitute that new, acceptable behavior for the old, less-wanted one.

Mrs. Roberts had no particular complaints about her eleven-year-old son, Hank. He was a responsible boy who could be depended on to follow his parents' instructions. He was always willing to assist in the care of his two younger sisters, and there was no serious rivalry between Hank and the girls. He was what many parents would term the ideal son, with one exception: he would *not* keep his room clean without persistent prodding. Any day Hank's room could be found with clothes lying on his bed (which was unmade), shoes scattered across the floor, school materials strewn about, and toys anywhere but in the toy box. Mrs. Roberts had tried coercion and force to teach him to consistently clean and straighten his bedroom, without success.

Following a discussion with her husband, Mrs. Roberts developed a plan to get Hank to substitute cleanliness for messiness in his room. It was normal for her children to complete specified chores around the house and yard. From time to time Mr. and Mrs. Roberts would confer with their children to make any necessary changes in their assignments. It was at such a conference that Mrs. Roberts informed Hank of a new responsibility she wanted him to consider.

"Hank, I've been thinking about increasing your status around the house. I've always counted on you to help me out in special ways and now I want to give you a duty that would be a big help to me."

"What's that?" Hank's curiosity had been aroused.

"I'd like you to be the bedroom supervisor for our family," continued Mother.

"What would I do?" Hank liked the title of supervisor.

"I've developed a checklist that I'd like you to complete three times each week. As a bedroom supervisor you would check each bedroom in the house to see that each of the jobs on the checklist has been properly done. That includes your bedroom, the girls' bedroom, and Dad's and my bedroom." Mrs. Roberts then presented her checklist that called for Hank to inspect whether or not the beds in each room had been made, clothes were hung in the closet, dresser top was neatly arranged, and the like. Hank looked it over and began to feel important.

"You say I get to inspect yours and Dad's room, too?"

"That's right. You inspect all of the bedrooms. Dad and I think you can handle the job. What do you think?"

"You've just hired a new supervisor!" came the enthusiastic response.

By mutual consent among the family members, bedroom inspections were scheduled for each Monday, Thursday, and Saturday. Dutifully, Hank checked each bedroom, including his own, and filed a report with his parents concerning the condition of each room, with recommendations for improvements. Not surprisingly, Hank's own bedroom was seldom found to be in disarray. He had replaced his maintaining an untidy room with a new role and a new reason for keeping his room neat and clean most of the time. Mrs. Roberts had changed her son's undesirable behavior by substituting another behavior that was directly opposite to it. Her method of introducing the new behavior was creative and represented positive behavioral modification. Hank's reward for keeping his room clean was inherent in the task, and it was reinforced by his knowing that he was performing his duty responsibly.

A second form of behavior substitution is to develop and reinforce acceptable behaviors to occupy time that the child may otherwise spend in unacceptable acts. While the positive behavior may not be directly opposite to the negative one, the two cannot be performed at the same time.

Sylvia was at it again! Late every afternoon before supper she was likely to make trouble. One day a neighbor down the street called her mother to complain that for the second time in the past few days she had caught Sylvia ringing her doorbell and running away in glee. The neighbor explained that the girl's behavior was harmless, but it created a nuisance nonetheless.

Sylvia's mother correctly surmised that since Sylvia had nothing to do in the late afternoon except create mischief, she needed a regular, organized activity. After they discussed a variety of alternatives, Sylvia decided to enroll in a gymnastics program for children at a neighborhood fitness center. Classes were held weekly after school, and students were encouraged to work out several times a week at home.

Sylvia liked the exercise program and made several new friends in the process. Because many of her afternoons were occupied by her sports activities, she was no longer free to roam around and annoy the neighbors. Her mother was relieved to have no more complaints.

While participation in an athletic program could not be considered the opposite of creating mischief in the neighborhood, the two activities could not be performed at the same time. Participating in an organized activity was a substitute for pestering the neighbors, which Sylvia had lost the opportunity to do.

Finally, substituting one behavior for another is a form of prevention. A teacher teaching cursive handwriting to a class of eight-year-olds will make every effort to teach the proper formation of letters to avoid having to retrain later on. Likewise, an athletic coach will logically train an athlete in the fundamental skills of a sport before teaching higher level skills. So, too, a parent can identify undesirable behaviors before they develop and thereby prevent the more difficult task of later eliminating them by teaching the desirable behaviors at the outset.

Seven-year-old Roy had just moved into a new neighborhood with his family. He had been at his new school only for a few days when he came home and told his mother of a fight that had taken place between two boys in his classroom. Following his description of the event, his mother remarked, "Those two boys must have been upset with one another to have gotten into a fight."

"I don't think they were really that mad, Mom. I think they just like to fight," reflected Roy.

"That's odd that they would choose to fight rather than settle their differences in some other way."

"Well, the other kids say that the big boy, Bobby, picks on everybody."

"Roy, what would you do if Bobby started to pick on you?" Mother asked.

"I'd tell him I don't want to fight."

"Suppose he called you a sissy?"

"I still wouldn't fight. I'd just walk off and stay away from him."

"What would be some other things you could do?" continued Mother.

"Well, I could hang around the nicer kids, or I could report it to my teacher. Or he might be willing to just talk it out."

"I think you really mean it that you don't want to fight, Roy. The answers you gave were very smart answers. It sounds like you've really thought about this." His mother showed her approval for his responsible answers to her questions.

While a parent cannot be certain that a discussion of a potential problem situation will prevent an undesirable behavior, such an exercise can teach and even reward an acceptable behavior before it takes place. Roy's mother wanted to prevent the rather common childhood behavior of fighting before it developed. Her questioning of her son allowed him to mentally rehearse several possible substitute behaviors for fighting. She then reinforced his response by showing her approval. If she had felt it necessary, she could have offered her own alternative behaviors to those he had provided and told how she might act in the same situation. Should a situation develop in the future in which Roy had to consider fighting, his prior training would help him make a positive, acceptable decision as to how to handle it.

*The rod of correction imparts
wisdom, but a child left to itself
disgraces his mother
(PROV. 29:15 NIV).*

# 19

# A Critique of Punishment

Ask parents what they do in response to their children's misbehavior and the answer will almost invariably be some type of punishment. It is a common thought that in order to teach children lessons about appropriate behavior it is necessary to spank, scold, or take away a privilege following an unacceptable act. Parents who resort primarily to the punishment technique of controlling children are usually unsuccessful and teach their children little about self-control in the long run.

Mrs. Leonard was visiting one afternoon at her friend's house. Because both ladies had three-year-old children, Mrs. Leonard was invited to bring along her daughter, Rebecca. As the two friends chatted, the children played peaceably in the playroom for about twenty minutes. Suddenly, Mrs. Leonard heard Rebecca complaining loudly and crying. She rushed to the playroom to see Rebecca standing over her playmate attempting to yank a toy from his grasp.

"Rebecca! What are you doing?" Mrs. Leonard was

embarrassed to see her daughter fighting with her host.

"Dickie won't let me have that doll bottle, and I want it!" whined her daughter.

"I had it first!" explained Dickie, still clutching the toy.

Mother spoke firmly to Rebecca. "Young lady, you let him have that toy—right now!"

"No! I want it!"

Mrs. Leonard took more drastic action, since her daughter did not obey her command. She reached down and slapped the youngster sharply on the hand and emphasized her point once again. "Stop it! Dickie can play with it. He had it first. You must learn to share!"

"But, Mommie . . ." Rebecca began to whine.

Mother pointed her finger in the girl's face. "Do you want another spanking?" she asked, fully knowing the answer.

"No." Rebecca pushed out her bottom lip and began to pout.

"Then this had better not happen again." She stared sternly at Rebecca for a moment and left the room. Only a few minutes later, the ruckus resumed in the playroom. Mrs. Leonard, knowing the probable cause of the disturbance, excused herself and made her way to the children to find her daughter once again attempting to commandeer a toy from Dickie.

"Rebecca, what did I tell you a few minutes ago?" demanded Mother.

"I want that bottle!" was the response.

Mrs. Leonard felt that she had a justifiable reason to spank her daughter and once again reached down and slapped her hands. Rebecca began to cry even louder. "But Mommie . . ."

"Rebecca, I told you this would happen if you argued with Dickie. I'll spank you again if I hear any more fussing and fighting from you," interrupted Mother.

As she rejoined her hostess, Mrs. Leonard apologized

for her actions. She explained herself by saying, "Sometimes I really have to be hard on her before she gets the message that I mean business."

Was Mrs. Leonard correct in her assessment of her struggle with Rebecca? Perhaps we should look for some of the actual messages Rebecca did receive from her mother through this attempt at modifying her behavior.

I think it is safe to say that Rebecca knew something about her behavior had caused her mother to be angry with her. That is, she had created a problem for her mother. Because it was a problem that Mrs. Leonard would not likely disregard, Rebecca had attracted her mother's undivided attention. Yet, Mrs. Leonard failed to actually identify the specific behavior that needed to be attacked. She simply attacked Rebecca. Thus, one message Rebecca received was that at that moment her mother did not like her. At the very least, her mother had no respect for her. Mother's tone of voice conveyed judgment. And the verdict? Guilty!

A second message Rebecca received was that as long as Mother did not find out about her misbehavior, she would receive no punishment. The second time she left the playroom, Mrs. Leonard said that if she heard Rebecca argue again, she would spank her again. The implication was, "It's all right to argue if I don't hear you. Just don't let me catch you!" Mrs. Leonard failed to foster in her daughter a sense of responsibility for her own action. She sent the message to her daughter that she would be responsible if she was *not* caught being irresponsible.

A third communication in the exchange was the assertion of the power of Mrs. Leonard over her daughter. In chapter 2 we examined the traditional view of the parent as the autocratic leader of the family, with the child having less worth than the adult. I maintained that parents and children should be looked on as equals in the sense that *both* are deserving of an equal share of respect and responsibility in the home. By doling out punishment in regular doses, Mrs. Leonard actually denied Rebecca the opportunity to gain a sense of personal responsibility for her own behavior. Mother assumed control of her daughter's actions and diminished the child's sense of worth.

Fourth, Mrs. Leonard encouraged Rebecca to attach negative characteristics to her mother. By associating emotions such as anger, disgust, and resentment to her mother's actions, Rebecca would over a period of time come to see these traits as being descriptive of her. It is quite possible that she actually would eventually avoid contact with her mother. A child who is punished on a regular basis by her parents will develop an internal conflict. Our society teaches us from an early age the importance of close family ties. Children, because of their relative dependency on their parents, are virtually forced into at least minimal contact with their parents. But discomfort may result in the child when she is in the presence of her punitive parent. Then guilt feelings grow as the child experiences negative emotions toward the one person to whom our culture demands that we give our allegiance—the parent.

Finally, the use of punishment has taught Rebecca that it is okay to fight back. She did something that her mother did not like (argue with her friend), and Mrs. Leonard retaliated by spanking her. Rebecca was nonverbally told that it is acceptable to strike out at those who oppose you. There are very few delinquent children or adults who did not receive this message loud and clear from their parents. They have been told that getting even or giving what one deserves is preferable to cooperation and reasonable action.

Now let's change the story of Mrs. Leonard and Rebecca and the communication between them. Mrs. Leonard and her hostess were chatting in the living room while Rebecca and Dickie played in the playroom.

Rebecca was heard complaining loudly and crying. Mrs. Leonard walked to the playroom and found Rebecca and her friend struggling over a favored toy.

"What happened, kids?" Mother attempted to find out what the problem was.

"Dickie won't let me have the doll bottle, and I want it!" whined Rebecca.

"I had it first!" protested Dickie.

Mother leaned over and calmly separated the two young warriors. Focusing upon her daughter, she explained, "Rebecca, fighting with Dickie is not acceptable. You may choose to play nicely with him or you may sit in the bathroom for five minutes. Which do you choose?"

"But, Mother, I want to play with the doll bottle," reiterated Rebecca.

"Rebecca, you may choose to play nicely with Dickie or you may sit in the bathroom for five minutes. Which do you choose?" repeated Mother.

"I'll play with Dickie," Rebecca decided.

"That's fine," agreed Mother. She then returned to the living room to rejoin her friend in conversation.

In this instance, Mrs. Leonard refrained from the use of punishment and avoided a struggle for dominance or power with Rebecca. She made no demands on the girl and passed no judgment on her. She did not suggest to Rebecca that she was angry with her behavior, although she did state a ground rule by commenting that fighting was unacceptable. By doing so, she communicated a principle to follow whether or not Mother was present. By giving Rebecca a choice, she did not invite disobedience or rebellion. Rebecca herself decided what her next action would be. Once Mother had completed her exchange with Rebecca she was able to walk away without the title of villain hanging over her head. She had talked in a frank, matter-of-fact manner with her daughter, but had not shown a lack of respect or threatened to withdraw her love. She had managed to remain neutral throughout the exchange.

Finally, Mrs. Leonard had managed to remain objective and settle the problem situation with Rebecca and Dickie without becoming emotional or overly involved in her daughter's predicament. Rather than turn the situation into a major struggle, she turned it into a learning experience for her daughter and indirectly told Rebecca that she was responsible for her own behavior.

*But the wisdom from above is first
pure, then peaceable, gentle, open to
reason, full of mercy and good
fruits, without uncertainty or
insincerity*
(JAMES 3:17 RSV).


# 20

# Who Owns the Problem?


Following the last chapter, the reader may be asking,
"Should children never be punished? Isn't part of life
learning to take the consequences of your actions?"

The answer is a resounding yes, but there is an important distinction between punishment and consequences.
Punishments are chosen and inflicted by parents on their
children. Consequences, on the other hand, are either
natural or previously agreed-upon outcomes of children's
behavior, and are based on the behaviors they have chosen. In this chapter we shall see that children learn best
from making their own choices of behavior and the
results—call it choosing their own positive or negative
reinforcements, if you will.

It was fifteen minutes until eight o'clock on a weekday
morning, and Mrs. Hardin was due to be at work in thirty
minutes. Her husband had already left for work, and she
was responsible for taking five-year-old Marcus to his
school. As she hurried to get ready to leave the house,
she decided to check on her son to see if he was ready
for school.

"Marcus? Are you ready yet?" called Mom.

"I couldn't find my socks and shoes."

Mrs. Hardin walked into the den to find Marcus sitting on the floor watching television. He obviously was not concerned about the time.

"Marcus, why are you just sitting there? Go find your school shoes. There are socks in your drawer. Get a pair that matches your clothes."

Marcus got up from the floor, walked into his bedroom, and took a cursory look around the room. The only shoes he saw were a pair of old sneakers. He grabbed a pair of red socks out of the dresser drawer and put those on as well as the sneakers. As he walked into his mother's bedroom, he stuck out one foot and asked, "Mom, would you tie my shoe?"

Mrs. Hardin looked down at Marcus's socks and shoes with horror. "I certainly will not! Where on earth did you find those socks and shoes? You can't wear *that* to school."

Marcus defended himself. "But Mom, you told me to get some socks and shoes and put them on. I was just doing what you told me."

Mrs. Hardin was disgusted at Marcus and becoming more frantic about the time. "Oh, Marcus, those socks don't match your clothes, and I wanted you to wear your school shoes—not those! Come here with me." She took Marcus by the hand and led him to his bedroom. After a thorough search of the room, she finally located his school shoes and a pair of socks that matched his clothes.

"Marcus, you realize this is causing us to be late this morning, don't you?" Marcus simply hung his head. "Yes, ma'am," he replied.

"You've got to stop being so poky in the mornings. We can't be late like this every day. I'll get in trouble with my boss if this happens too many times."

After finally getting herself and Marcus readied, Mrs. Hardin and her son rushed out of the house. Neither person was in a good mood by then, and both were late arriving at school and work.

This scene at the Hardin household was doomed to repeat itself. While outward circumstances may change from incident to incident, a regular pattern of behavior is well established. First of all, a problem situation arises. In this case Marcus was without matching socks and clean shoes. Second, Mother fails to accept her son's efforts to solve his problems on his own. She was not about to allow him to enter his classroom wearing play shoes and socks that did not match his clothes. Third, Mother takes the burden of Marcus's problem on her own shoulders and begrudgingly solves it for him. In doing so, she has rejected his actions and left him feeling incompetent and dependent on others to take responsibility for his behavior.

One of the primary mistakes parents make is to act *for* their children and make decisions for them. When this happens, numerous negative messages are sent to the children. The most obvious outcome is the youngsters' sense of rejection. In the illustration above, Marcus was told in various ways that his solution to the problem of finding socks and shoes to wear was a poor one. He was also blamed for his mother being late for work.

Furthermore, in most instances in which the parent takes a problem away from a child and solves it for him, negative emotions are expressed in the interchange between the two. You can imagine the tone of voice Mrs. Hardin used as she spoke to Marcus. She probably spoke sharply, with resentment and frustration in her voice. She certainly was not smiling throughout the ordeal, but likely wore a frown on her face. While she did not directly say it, she communicated a judgment against Marcus for his irresponsible behavior.

We parents are frequently unwilling to allow our children to experience the natural results or consequences of their behavior. We tend to become too absorbed in our own concerns of how our child's behavior will reflect on us and fail to consider the emotional needs of our children. Mrs. Hardin would have felt punished if Marcus had gone to school wearing red socks and old sneakers. Marcus's problem of having to find shoes and socks to wear became *her* problem.

A major aim of managing children's behavior should be to teach them to be responsible for their own behavior. It is unnecessary for parents to solve all problems that confront their children. Parents do well to allow children to choose their behaviors (within certain limits) and then allow them to learn from their choices.

The Sterling household was no different from most other normal homes. The family included three children who got along relatively well, but argued and fought from time to time. One of the most common arguments centered around which evening television shows they would watch. The disagreement was usually solved by Mom or Dad who took the problem into their own hands and decided which show would get the nod. As might be expected, there was always grumbling about the selection. In an effort to be fair, Mom and Dad generally tried to show an impartial attitude by alternately choosing the favorite show of each child. Even this scheme, however, was unsuccessful, because the siblings usually could not agree on whose show they had watched last.

After receiving counsel concerning a more effective means of dealing with this situation, the Sterlings told their children of their new approach to selecting the television show.

"Kids, if you can come to an agreement tonight on which show you would like to watch, you may watch TV. If you choose to argue about which show you will watch, then the TV may not be turned on all evening. Does everybody understand the choices?" All three children nodded that they understood. To insure, however, that they knew beyond a shadow of a doubt what the alternatives were, he repeated them. "If you can agree without arguing on the show you would like to watch, you may watch TV tonight. If you choose to argue about which show you will watch, then you have chosen not to watch TV." Once again everyone nodded.

Not more than a half hour later, one of the Sterling children flipped on the TV set, and immediately the other two cast a vote for their favorite show. Within a matter of seconds there was an argument. Hearing the commotion, Dad walked into the living room and quietly turned off the television set.

"Dad, we wanted to watch TV!" came the protest from all three children.

"I realize that you wanted to watch TV, but since you have chosen to argue about which show you will watch, you have chosen not to watch TV tonight," explained Dad in a calm tone of voice.

"It's okay if we watch what Mickey and Janie want to watch. We won't argue anymore," pleaded Jerry, the youngest of the three.

"I'm sorry, kids, but you have chosen not to watch TV," repeated Dad, matter-of-factly. With those words he left the room and the children did not watch television.

The following evening, Mickey approached his dad on behalf of his siblings. "Dad, may we watch TV tonight?"

Once again, Mr. Sterling explained, "If you can agree without arguing about which show you will watch, you may watch TV. If you choose to argue, then the television may not be turned on all evening."

Mickey quickly reported back to his brother and sister. "He said we can watch TV if we don't argue."

"Then let's not argue," suggested Janie. "There's a show I want to watch tonight."

"What show is that?" inquired Mickey. Janie named the show. "Is that all right with you, Jerry?" Mickey asked his brother.

"I guess. It beats nothing."

Having made a decision without argument, they walked into the living room, turned on the television and watched the selected show. After turning on the set Mickey looked at his dad. "How's that, Dad?"

"I see you chose a TV show to watch without arguing."

"Yep," came the reply.

In his management of his children's undesirable behavior (arguing over television viewing), Mr. Sterling successfully avoided the most dangerous pitfall; he refused to take away from his children the problem they had created. Rather than continue in the pattern of breaking up their argument and negotiating a settlement among them, he provided them alternatives and allowed them to choose how they would act. His only obligation in the matter was to ensure that the behavior they chose was accompanied by the established consequence. He allowed them to make their own choice, while he remained neutral on the matter.

On the first day of the new arrangement, Mr. Sterling was immediately put to the test when his children argued over which show they would view. He correctly followed through with the consequences of the children's choice of behavior and turned off the television set. He then politely refused his son's pleading to allow them to reconsider. By doing so, he communicated to them that he would no longer assume responsibility for their actions, but would follow through with the *first* choice they had made. Had he given them a second chance he would have clearly communicated a willingness (once again) to become involved in *their* problem and would have failed to teach them responsible behavior.

Also of importance in the successful transfer of a problem back to its original source is the general demeanor and sense of composure that is maintained by the parent. In our illustration, Mr. Sterling presented the choices to his children in a calm and rational manner. He refrained from emphasizing one alternative over the other or from explaining the merits of the preferred choice. When his children chose by their actions not to watch television, he did not moralize with his children, preach to them, or tell them "I told you so." After all, he was neutral on the matter of which alternative they selected.

Had he chosen to show negative *or* positive responses to the youngsters, he would have communicated a willingness to emotionally invest himself in *their* decision and would have once again become a part owner of their problem. A negative response to the children such as "All right, I told you all *not* to argue, and you didn't listen! I'm turning the TV off!" carries with it a sense of punishment for their selection and suggests a lack of respect for their own action. Parents must maintain their distance from the problems. Their only obligation is to accept the choices that the children make.

*And what does the LORD require of you?*
*To act justly, and to love mercy,*
*and to walk humbly with your God*
(MIC. 6:8 NIV).

# 21

# You're on Stage

Many teenagers would laugh at the suggestion that they are very much like either of their parents. Their argument would be based on the worlds of difference between themselves and Mom or Dad. I recently discussed this very issue with an adolescent boy who told me, "There's no way my dad and I are alike! He hates the music I listen to. He jokes about the clothes I wear. He thinks my friends are odd. He wishes I loved to watch golf on TV with him. When we go someplace together, we don't have much to say to each other. You're crazy to think that my father and I are alike! We're completely different."

The boy was wrong. From his father he had learned to be a top-flight critic of others. He was very talkative and sociable, just like his dad. Both placed high importance on the opinions others had of them, were stingy with their money, and so the list went on.

Psychologists have learned a great deal about the effect of adult modeling on the behavior of children. The success of a behavior management system in the home depends on the way parents demonstrate the principles, attitudes, and beliefs they verbally encourage.

Even though observers of human behavior in Aristotle's day recognized the influence of models on learning, the study of this form of learning was not taken seriously until the middle of this century. It has now been shown that we are mistaken to believe that children's behavior is changed solely as a result of punishment or reinforcers.

Mr. and Mrs. McNeil were exasperated over the behavior of their teenaged daughter, Melody. Melody had been a relatively easy child to get along with until the last two or three years. Since her entry into adolescence, however, new problems seemed to develop daily. She was in danger of failing school for the first time in her life. Whereas she formerly was good about completing her tasks, she could no longer be counted on to follow even the simplest request. The arguments between Melody and her parents, especially Mom, had drastically increased. Mr. and Mrs. McNeil had just about decided that their daughter was a lost cause.

Melody told a different story. She readily admitted to many of the behaviors her parents had described. She regretted the fact that her grades in school were on a downward slide. But, she firmly believed that she was justified in acting as she did.

Melody's argument was that she was acting as her parents acted. She related that her mother was habitually late for work and had, in fact, been threatened with the loss of her job for her excessive tardiness and poor work performance. She accused her mother of being irresponsible in the way she assumed her own household duties. Furthermore, Melody felt compelled to argue with her mom because of the persistent nagging she received.

Counseling sessions ensued in which emphasis was placed on the mother-daughter relationship. Mrs. McNeil was stunned as she heard her daughter describe her as a role model. She was unaware of the scrutiny under which Melody had placed her. After several sessions marked by openness and honesty, changes were made in the behavior of both Mrs. McNeil and Melody. Mrs. McNeil was pleased to discover that her own growth as an individual meant that her daughter had a healthier model to follow.

Just how strong is the modeling effect on our children? How much do our children learn by observation? It is interesting to discuss these questions in the light of children's developmental stages of thought. Young children think in very concrete terms. They do not analyze the behavior of others in great detail, for they are incapable of that type of thinking. Thus, young children will imitate their parents without a full understanding of their reasons for doing so.

As they grow into adolescence, however, children become more capable of interpreting the behavior of others. Thirteen-year-olds, for instance, analyze the motives behind their parents' behavior and then apply its usefulness to themselves. They are no longer simply imitating Mom or Dad; they now study their parents and imitate selectively.

Herbert was an adolescent who categorized himself as different from his mother in many ways. He felt completely separate from her and had little to do with her. Yet, despite his physical and emotional distance from his mother, he had learned a great deal from observing her over his sixteen years.

Herbert's mom kept her thoughts to herself. She had few close friends, but was well thought of within the community. She was a deeply religious woman who unintentionally forced her beliefs on Herbert, steadfastly hoping that he would accept her system of beliefs in due time. Despite her convictions, she struggled in many areas of her own life. Her marriage to Herbert's father was poor, largely because of her insistence that he conform to her rigid standards of behavior. Again, she believed that in time her husband would come to his senses and accept her unspoken demands. Maintaining a conversation of depth and meaning was difficult for this woman. She refused to acknowledge the crumbling family relations and the increasing problems that engulfed her son.

Herbert, though he felt as a stranger to his mother, had learned much from her about how to face life's problems. He was now deeply depressed. At the root of his depression was anger, much of which was aimed at his mother. He resented her withholding the opportunity for him to express his thoughts and feelings over the years.

Yet, despite his very obvious despair and sadness, Herbert adamantly denied being depressed. He maintained that in time he would leave home and have only limited contact with his parents, thus making his life more gratifying. He, too, had a poor relationship with his father, yet would not acknowledge the severity of this crippled alliance. His thinking was that by ignoring it, the relationship would either improve or eventually dissolve on its own. Like his mother, he had a wide range of associates, but precious few individuals to call his friends.

Herbert had not developed these behaviors in a vacuum. Many of them were learned through his lack of communication skills and his having no close friendships with others nor a desire for intimacy. His belief that things would eventually get better without any effort at relationship building and his denial of his own serious depression mirrored his mom's denial of the existence of her own personal dissatisfaction. She, in turn, was unaware of the influence she had on her son through her actions and attitudes. Her desire to see her son make changes in his behavior was strangled by her constant model of denial, dissatisfaction, and rigidity.

If a poor role model has such a potent influence on the

development of negative behaviors and attitudes in children, imagine the usefulness of a good one in encouraging positive behavior. Because of the teachable nature of young children, it is prudent to provide ample opportunity for them to observe in parents desirable behavioral skills and attitudes.

Mrs. Merrill had been having an increasingly difficult time with six-year-old Mike. He was the youngest of four children and accustomed to being the center of attention—too accustomed, in fact. When Mike's mother made a request of him, whether to hang his clothes in the closet, eat his vegetables, or take a bath, he was likely to respond by throwing a tantrum or by screaming, "I don't have to do what you tell me to do," or "Go ahead and make me," or "Do it yourself."

Mrs. Merrill was perplexed. She didn't know what to do with Mike to get him to comply with her reasonable demands of him. She discussed the matter with her husband, who reminded her that Mike liked her very much. The couple reasoned that Mike had become virtually addicted to Mom's attention and threw tantrums and screamed as a way of ensuring that he got the notice he desired. His plan was working to perfection!

As the parents analyzed Mike's behavior, they realized that he had been given no training in this area of social skills, that is, of complying with the simple requests made of him by adults.

Mr. and Mrs. Merrill discussed with Mike and his siblings their plan of action. Mike was told that he had two new behaviors to learn. The first was to listen to instructions so he would understand what he was to do. His second was to do exactly what he was told to do.

Mike was then told that the successful completion of these tasks would result in a reinforcement for him. He would be recognized regularly in a positive way when he demonstrated compliance to authority figures. The consequence would be isolation by his parents if the task was not completed. But the plan did not stop there.

Mr. and Mrs. Merrill enlisted two of Mike's older siblings to do some role playing for Mike to watch. His oldest sister, Michelle, and brother, Mitchell, enacted a scene in which complying with a request was required. Mitchell listened attentively as Michelle gave him a simple task to perform. He then willingly followed through with the assignment without displaying a negative attitude. Michelle reinforced the behavior of her actor brother by hugging him and asking him to spend time with her in play activity.

The family then discussed the skit. Simple questions were directed to Mike. "How should you behave when an adult tells you to do something?" "What did Mitchell do when Michelle made a request of him?" "How did Michelle feel when Mitchell did as she asked?" "How did Mitchell feel?" Mike was beginning to get the idea of what was expected of him.

But, still, the plan had more components. Over the next weeks each family member made a concerted effort to respect the reasonable requests made by other family members. Mom and Dad listened to their children and followed their reasonable requests as models of the behavior they desired to see in their kids. They followed through consistently with either rewards or consequences when Mike was given instructions. They successfully capitalized on Mike's observation of their behavior and on his capacity to learn from their renewed efforts to reinforce his appropriate behavior. Informal discussions about Mike's progress were held periodically, with an occasional practice session to encourage the continued development of this social skill.

Good social skills are needed if a child is to become responsible, productive, and satisfied in life, and developing them should be a goal of a behavior management system. Teaching appropriate behavior is an ongoing process. Correction, punishment, and manipulating the child's environment are only tools to implement change. The probability of maintaining new, appropriate behaviors increases substantially as these behaviors are modeled by the parents.

PART **3**

# Effective
# Communication

*Whatever is true, whatever is
honorable, whatever is just,
whatever is pure, whatever is lovely,
whatever is gracious, if there is any
excellence, if there is anything
worthy of praise, think on these
things*
(PHIL. 4:8 RSV).

# 22

# Learn to Listen

Mrs. Barfield and Mrs. Thomas were enjoying a morning cup of coffee together. Both mothers had teen-aged children and both were perplexed about how to communicate with their children. "One of the things I don't understand," explained Mrs. Barfield, "is that my daughter will take several minutes to tell me something and when she's through telling me, if I make even one simple suggestion, she complains that I'm not listening to her."

"I hear the same thing from my son. I don't know when to say something to him, or when to keep quiet. He always says that I don't understand him."

The first step in improving communications with children is to learn to listen to them. "Listen?" you say. "My child talks so much I can't help but listen!"

My first point in discussing the art of communication is to distinguish the term *hearing* from *listening*. Children are heard when their words are absorbed by their parents' auditory senses. Hearing is physical. Listening, on the other hand, is to understand the spoken messages and the more-difficult-to-detect unspoken or hidden messages.

The major cause of poor communication between a parent and child comes from the parent's tendency to focus on the surface of the child's words. That is, many parents choose to merely hear their children. The good listener, on the other hand, discerns and responds to the thoughts, needs, and emotions contained but hidden in the spoken words.

Gene came home from school late one afternoon with a long look on his face. He walked into the house and glanced at his mother, but did not say a word. As he headed for his bedroom, Mother spoke up.

"Hello, Gene," she said in a pleasant voice. "Glad you could make it home."

"Yeah, sorry I'm a little late," mumbled Gene. "That stupid girl, Penny!" he suddenly blurted out. "She acts like she likes me, but when I try to talk to her, she just acts dumb and won't say anything. That makes me think she doesn't like me and then I feel foolish for even talking to her in the first place!"

"Well, Gene," said Mother in a consoling tone of voice, "you'll probably have a lot of foolish moments like that before you grow up."

"Then I don't want to grow up," snapped Gene and stomped to his bedroom.

His mother was dumbfounded at his poor attitude toward her. At the very time she attempted to console her son, he flatly rejected her. Gene had a need and desire to be listened to by a responsible adult, which his Mother sensed the moment he walked into the house wearing a long face. She was initially receptive and made a statement to try to cheer him. Her light comment, "Hello, Gene. Glad you could make it home," was her attempt to break the ice with her son and make him feel at ease.

Gene took his mother's words as an indication that

she would listen to and understand his feelings of the moment. In a release of frustration and emotion, he explained to his mother his difficulties in understanding and effectively communicating with a girl whom he admired, thereby immediately revealing his feelings to his mother.

But look what happened! Gene's mother made one statement, and the conversation was ended. Did her words have a magic appeal that caused Gene to immediately feel a sense of relief in unburdening his problem? Certainly not. Gene made a quick judgment that his mother was not likely to fulfill his need to be listened to and understood. Of course he knew that this would not be the only time he would feel foolish during his lifetime. Mother's statement was superficial as far as Gene was concerned. Seeing that the door to an understanding listener was closed, he quickly withdrew from her presence. In the exchange between Gene and his mother, she had focused primarily on the words her son had spoken and not on the underlying emotions and feelings that he needed to communicate.

Communication between a parent and child stops when a parent makes a response that is irrelevant, sarcastic, or meaningless. It is amazing how quickly children and adolescents can detect a poor listener. Then, those who cannot satisfactorily express themselves orally will always find other ways to convey their feelings to the world. They may throw temper tantrums or withdraw. Abnormal behaviors such as thumbsucking or excessive rocking are often expressions of unspoken emotions.

Randle was a ten-year-old boy. He had many good qualities about him. He was handsome, made good grades in school, got along well with other children, and conversed easily with adults. His father was a professional man who was in good standing in the community. His mother was active in community affairs. Randle had an older brother he was close to and with whom he played in a congenial manner.

Despite all his positive characteristics, Randle had a major behavioral problem. Almost every day for two years he had soiled his pants. This habit had begun almost overnight and showed no signs of ending. His parents were perplexed. They had tried almost everything they could think of to remedy the problem. They had spanked their son for his accidents, but no improvement was noted. They took away privileges for his action, but this did not faze him. They even bought him presents or gave him special treats on the occasional days he correctly used the toilet. Still no change was seen. In despair they came to my office for help.

After visiting with Randle and his mother and father several times, a clear picture began to come into focus. Although Mom and Dad had an outwardly sound marriage, there were many hidden problems. Dad was secretly dissatisfied with his work and did not enjoy his profession. Yet, because of his age and the number of years he had invested in his job, he did not feel he could afford to make a career change. He spent long hours at his office and often came home in a foul mood. He expressed his displeasure with his work situation by being sarcastic toward his sons and often bickering with his wife. He lacked energy much of the time and only halfheartedly fulfilled his responsibilities around the house. He occasionally participated in activities with his sons, but not on a routine basis. For him, life had lost its excitement.

Mom, on the other hand, was found to be a cool, emotionally hardened but busy woman. When she was not active in the community, she was active at home. Her most dominating personality characteristic was her perfectionism. She insisted on doing everything in precisely the right manner. There was no middle ground and no room for error. Her relationship with her two sons and her husband was marked by her demands for a high level of performance. She did not tolerate a job poorly done, whether it was making the bed or preparing an elaborate meal for dinner guests.

Communication between these parents and Randle was in shambles. Randle found he could not talk to either of his parents; they were preoccupied with their own worries. It was useless to attempt to communicate with Dad, because he was too frequently buried in unhappiness. Mom could not be counted on to listen to his concerns because she was too demanding and emotionally aloof. Randle enjoyed his older brother, but he was just a kid, too, and was not mature enough to be of assistance to his little brother.

Randle was an unhappy boy. He badly wanted to feel nurtured and loved by Mom and Dad, so his only alternative was to express himself through some type of nonverbal means. The method he subconsciously chose was soiling his clothes.

As Randle's parents began to understand their relationship with their son, they were able to recognize opportunities to listen to him and attend to his needs. Randle continued to receive counseling and eventually saw that other people did, indeed, take time to listen to him. He saw that his mother and father were noticing his verbal and nonverbal emotional expressions. He came to believe that he could talk to them about many topics and genuinely be listened to and understood. As time passed, Randle soiled his pants somewhat less frequently, then noticeably less frequently and finally the behavior ceased.

The atmosphere in his home had improved. Randle had room to grow, but most of all he could smile inwardly, because he knew he could talk and be listened to by his parents.

As we conclude our first chapter in this section on communication, I must re-emphasize the importance of the act of listening. In considering effective communication, it is important to first develop this skill, for it is the cornerstone of all communication.

Some specific exercises can help develop good listening talents. They can be done at any place and at any time of the day. A first exercise is to practice listening to your children or someone else's children. Without becoming involved in their activity, sit back and listen. Take notice of their words and ask yourself what thoughts, emotions, and feelings are coming through. You may choose to sit in a nearby chair and jot down these impressions.

Second, in your daily conversations with children, take note of your own verbal and nonverbal responses. Were your responses appropriate, or were they irrelevant? Did you tell the children what you thought they were feeling? Did the children abruptly end the conversations? What was your level of attention in each case? Did your facial expressions give away your disinterest, or did you look at the children while you listened to them?

Listening begins with awareness of our own behavior. Most parents have never focused on or thought about their own listening habits. Effective dialogue can take place only when listening gives it its meaning, and understanding its heart. Children who are assured they are worth being listened to will more likely behave in a worthy manner.

*When I was a child,*
*I talked like a child,*
*I thought like a child,*
*I reasoned like a child.*
*When I became a man I put*
*childish ways behind me*
(1 Cor. 13:11 niv).

# 23

## But I Have My Reasons

Parents are human. They really are! There are times that listening to a child seems virtually impossible. Burdens are so heavy that children are the last ones to receive the attention they need from their mother and father. There are common excuses and reasons for not listening to children. Let's examine several of the more popular ones.

It was Saturday at last, and Mother and Daddy had promised all week to take the children swimming that afternoon. As the parents and children were driving to the swimming pool, the children were saying precisely what they would do to entertain themselves in the water.

Joyce, at age nine, was the oldest of the trio of children. She had taken swimming lessons throughout the summer and was getting to be quite a fish in the water. Her level of excitement was high.

"Daddy, I'm going to show you how I can dive off the side of the pool into the water," she pronounced boldly.

"That's great. Is that something you've learned at your swimming lessons?"

"Yes, and I'm getting pretty good at it. My teacher says so."

"I can't wait to watch you. I'm sure you'll do well."

Once they arrived at the pool, the kids excitedly made their way into the water. Mother and Daddy got into the water with them. After a few minutes, Joyce hopped out of the water and stood along its edge, poised to dive back in.

"Watch, Daddy! I'm going to show you how I can dive. Are you watching?"

"I'm watching, honey. Go ahead and give it your best." Joyce leaped into the air, spread her arms out wide, and smacked the water in a perfect "belly buster." Despite her less-than-perfect dive, she surfaced with a smile on her face. She had done her best.

"Well, Daddy, how was that?" asked Joyce, expecting a favorable comment.

"Well, sugar, you did a belly buster. Didn't that hurt your stomach?"

"Shoot, no! Watch me dive again!" She got out of the water quickly and stood at the side. In a moment, she jumped into the pool and duplicated her less-than-picturesque dive. As she came up again, Daddy met her.

"Here, Joyce. Come over here and let me show you how to dive." Daddy got out of the water with Joyce and proceeded to instruct her in the art of diving.

"Now, the first thing you need to do is to bend your legs before you jump, like this." Daddy then demonstrated the technique.

"Like this?" asked Joyce as she crouched down low.

"No, no. You're stooping much too low. Don't bend down quite so far. See, look at me." Daddy demonstrated again as Joyce looked on with a certain sense of disgust.

"Okay, Daddy, I think I can do it," came the assured response. As she stooped down, Daddy squeezed her stomach in with one hand and pushed down on her back.

"Bend at the waist and look at the water," coached

Daddy, "and then just push off the side into the water. It's real simple. Okay, go ahead."

Joyce did the best she could and fell into the water. Even with the instruction she had just received on diving technique, her effort was not as good as the belly buster she was able to do on her own. When she broke through the water, she was not smiling but looked expectantly at her father, waiting for his judgment.

"Well, we have a way to go, but I think we can make some improvements. C'mon, let's try it again." Daddy was determined to teach his daughter to dive.

"I think I'll go swim with the other kids," came the unexpected response.

"But Joyce, you'll never learn to dive if you don't practice. And I'm willing to teach you. I think you'll get it before too long." Dad was eager to continue the lesson.

"That's okay. They look like they're having fun over there." Joyce then swam over to join several other children in their play.

As Daddy crawled back into the pool, he told his wife with a shake of the head, "She acts like she wants to learn to dive, but when I try to teach her, she won't try. She'll never learn anything with that kind of attitude."

Daddy was unaware that he had failed to listen to his daughter. The excited way she approached diving into the pool was her way of stating her personal pride in her ability. She was thrilled to be able to show her father a new trick. She nonverbally implied that she was happy to be at the swimming pool with her family and friends. Daddy had responded to none of that.

Yet he had a reason for his inattention to Joyce: he quickly became emotionally involved in her technique. He was not personally satisfied with her belly buster, and felt she could do a better job of diving. He reasoned that he could teach Joyce proper diving technique, and to do so became a goal for his own pride. Her problem was now his problem. He was no longer able to listen to Joyce, to hear her excitement or see her pleasure; he only heard the voice inside himself telling him what he could do to correct the problem. The end result? Communication between the two broke down and the child chose to be with her friends.

Certainly, having children to rear causes a great many emotions to well up inside a parent. The emotional attachment between parent and child is healthy and, of course, desirable. Too often, however, parents try to make children extensions of themselves. They may do this by being overly protective or excessively critical, or by closely directing the movements and thinking of their children. But, good listeners maintain objective outlooks toward each other. When parents replace objective listening by subjective goals, they hamper communication.

A second problem is that of interpersonal family conflict. It can easily be seen how poor personal relations between a parent and child may stand in the way of communication. It is also possible, however, for poor relations between a parent and other family members to be an excuse for poor listening.

Mr. and Mrs. Wilburn got along fairly well. They had been married more than twenty years, but the excitement of their relationship had long been gone. Oh, sure, they still loved each other, but there were many things that caused friction and irritation between them. One habit Mr. Wilburn had maintained throughout the years was that he enjoyed chewing on a toothpick after supper. Mrs. Wilburn often told her husband how crude she thought he looked with a toothpick hanging from the side of his mouth. She considered it a disgusting habit and barely tolerated him when he did it.

One evening the Wilburn's seventeen-year-old son, Norman, followed his dad's example and took a toothpick to his mouth. About a half hour later, Norman approached his mother.

"Hey, Mom, could you wash these brown slacks for

me? I want to wear them when I eat dinner at Debbie's house tomorrow night."

Mom turned toward her son and immediately noticed the toothpick in his mouth. In a flash she visualized Norman growing up with many of the same irritating characteristics as her husband. She could not bear to think of her son exhibiting such poor manners.

"Can't you think of something else to wear?" Mom snapped. "I don't think I'll have time to wash and dry a load of clothes tomorrow. You've got other clean slacks in your closet." With that, she turned away and walked into the den where her husband sat.

"What was that all about?" inquired Dad, who had heard Mrs. Wilburn's sharp remarks.

"Oh, Norman is developing bad habits just like yours," was the response.

In this instance, it was Mrs. Wilburn's resentment of her husband's habit that caused her to fail to listen to her son. Her snappy response was not actually meant to be a judgment against Norman. It was her strained relationship with Mr. Wilburn that was underscored by her words.

A third reason (there are more) for parents often failing to listen to their children is their own inner struggles. There are times the trials parents' offspring must face are so similar to their own they cannot listen to their children because they cannot bear to face their own problems.

Nick had experimented with an assortment of drugs and alcohol. He did not think he was unable to turn away from them, but he knew he was close to that point. In talking with me about his relationship with his family members, he said that he received support and encouragement from each, with the exception of his father. In discussing his father, he made several revealing statements.

"My father and I used to be pretty close," confided

Nick, "but over the last three or four years that has changed. We hardly ever talk to each other, and when we do talk, neither of us has much to say. I've gotten the feeling many times that my dad wants to ignore me, to pretend that I'm not there. I think he's afraid that I'll be just like him, and he can't stand that. He won't listen to me when I want to talk."

In a separate conference with Nick's dad, I found the boy's perception of the man proved to be very accurate. Although it was difficult for Dad to express himself, he stated that he had had trouble controlling his consumption of alcohol for quite some time. He would go for two or three weeks—even a month—without so much as a sip of alcohol, but he could never stay away from the drink any longer. Periodically he would consume great quantities and be little more than a drunkard for several days at a time.

Dad unsuccessfully tried to hide his problem and keep from others his feelings of inadequacy. In an emotional tone of voice, he explained, "I can't tell you how many times I've wanted to stop Nick from developing this habit. Yet, every time I've looked at him for the past two years, I see myself—and I don't like him. I don't want him to be like me, and I don't want to be near him."

It was this father's weakness that prevented his listening and helping his son. He was unable to control his own problems, and seeing them reflected in the boy was more than he could bear; therefore, he withdrew from him.

Effective communication begins with a willingness to recognize and set aside subjective feelings and enter the world of the child—to really listen. Real listening may be the most difficult but also the most important thing in communication.

*I will counsel you*
*and watch over you*
(Ps. 32:8 NIV).

# 24

# Now What Do I Say?

It is one thing to learn to listen to children, but another distinct skill is needed to communicate to them that you have indeed listened. Parents may fail in this because of their inappropriate choice of words. Every parent has been in a situation where the child says something and an appropriate response does not come to mind.

Louis was a fourteen-year-old boy who had been in and out of trouble during the previous two or three years. He had always been a mischievous child, even when young, but now a life-changing incident caused him to become more pensive and reflective.

One evening at a school athletic event, Louis and a buddy were roaming aimlessly about the parking lot. They were not interested in the athletic contest, but had come to the game because it was the place to be.

Suddenly, the two friends were confronted by several older boys. Although somewhat frightened, Louis was not intimidated by these bigger fellows. As a matter of fact, the entire situation was a little bit exciting to him.

The youths argued for a few minutes over a petty circumstance. Things quickly got out of hand, however, and Louis and his companion suddenly found themselves in an unexpected fight.

One of the older boys pulled a knife and threatened to use it maliciously on Louis and his friend. His friend helplessly watched as Louis was hurt physically and emotionally. Fortunately, a policeman stopped the boys before more serious harm was done.

Legal charges were filed against the boy. After several weeks he was brought before a juvenile court and given a stern warning and one year's probation.

Louis was disheartened by the judge's decision. He had hoped for a stiffer punishment for the youth who had harmed him. Additionally, he feared the incident would repeat itself, because the boy had a reason to begrudge Louis. On hearing of his assailant's light sentence, Louis said nothing and went home. As he arrived at home, however, the urge to express himself overwhelmed him. He found his mother and poured out his heart to her.

"It's not fair!" he protested. "I just heard that Grimes only got one year of probation. It's just not fair!"

Mother was taken by surprise at her son's news and did not know exactly how to respond to his outburst of anger. Quickly she replied, "Well, Louis, that's one lesson in life you'll have to learn. Everything's not always fair. That judge was just doing what he thought was right."

"But Mother, you don't understand! I don't think that judge understands how mean Grimes is. He should've sent him to reform school!"

"Louis, you can't say that! If they sent him off to a reform school, he'd probably come back meaner than ever."

"Well, I don't care," Louis replied angrily. "That judge was wrong!" With that he walked into his bedroom and wept bitter tears of hatred.

Louis had placed his mother in a difficult position. He had burst on her with an emotion-laden comment about the judge, and she had but a moment to decide on her response. Impulsively she simply stated what *she* felt about the judge's decision.

It's natural to respond to children, as well as adults, by stating our own opinion, position, or feeling. Doing so, however, signals the speaker that we are not paying full attention. But the primary objective in communicating with youngsters should always be to understand the problem from *their* point of view. It does children no good to hear their parent's interpretation of the story when their immediate need is to express themselves. Initially, they are not ready to come to a conclusion or reach an agreement. They have the right to feel as they do at that moment and to share their feelings with another concerned human being. Analysis and conclusions come later.

When Louis came home with a tremendous burden of anger, resentment, fear, and a host of other emotions, he needed to unburden them on a caring individual, not be consoled with a lesson about the ways of the world.

One way to let children know they have been genuinely understood is to as accurately as possible rephrase the emotion they have tried to put into words. The communication between Louis and his mother would have progressed to a deeper level if she had said something like, "So the judge was light on Grimes, and you don't think that is right. In fact, you're quite upset that the penalty was not stiffer." Louis would have known his mother had genuinely heard him and fully understood his feelings of that moment.

When children talk to their parents they need to know that any emotion they have will not be denied. Yet, adults tend to reject children's negative emotions such as anger, hatred, envy, jealousy, and fear. No doubt most adults got the same rejection from their own parents.

Negative emotions are generally perceived as too uncomfortable or improper. But these emotions are natural and legitimate. Indeed, if children suppress them by being allowed no verbal outlets, their thoughts and feelings will surface in the form of anxiety, misbehavior, depression, or the like.

As we discussed in chapter 2, every parent has a system of beliefs about the nature of children. Some parents see their children as naturally prone toward negative behavior and feel the need to "harness the lion," which leads them to deny their children's right to express negative thoughts. The underlying idea is that by disallowing expression of these thoughts, they will vanish and not dominate the child's behavior. But the opposite is true!

Louis's mother implied in her response that she did not believe it to be his right to think and say what he did, that his feelings were inappropriate, even though at a later point she may have been able to look back on the incident and understand her son's anger. When Louis said that Grimes should have been sent to reform school, Mother replied, "Louis, you can't say that!" The focus of their conversation thereby turned away from his frustration with the judge toward Mother's condemnation of his negative outburst. His response of walking away was predictable.

Parents willing to allow children to "own" their problems are guided by their belief that every child has the capability, with guidance, to develop positive characteristics. They are effective listeners. Louis was not yet ready to reach the conclusion that life is not always fair and that nothing could change what had taken place, although it is possible that in time he would have reached this conclusion on his own.

Mother, however, did not think he would be able to reach a reasonable conclusion on his own. Thus, she intervened and took his problem away from him, so to speak, and attempted to provide its solution: he would have to accept the fact that an injustice had been done. The door to further meaningful communication was slammed shut. Without an effective listener, Louis was then forced to wrestle the problem away from his mother and carry his heavy burden into his bedroom.

Listening parents are understanding parents who respond to their children's frame of reference instead of their own, skilled parents who communicate that understanding by correctly rephrasing the children's statements and thereby identifying with their feelings, bold parents who will allow their childen their rights to express any emotions, responsible parents who will not try to take their children's problems and solve them for them.

Fortunate are the children who are able to relate intimate thoughts to listening parents. Through such a relationship they are encouraged by their parents to reach responsible conclusions that will guide their future behavior.

*A soft answer quiets anger*
(PROV. 15:1 GNB).

# 25

# Keeping the Lines Open

Once your children are assured they have access to their parents' sympathetic ears, how do you keep the words flowing? And why is it important that you do?

It is necessary here to re-emphasize a point that has been made throughout this book: that much more is communicated from one person to another than the spoken words. Experts in the field of human communication tell us that the vast majority of those words carry hidden messages that go undetected by the listener who is not attuned to them.

During infancy and the early years children openly reveal their true thoughts and feelings to adults. As time passes, their verbal expressions become more guarded and they select only the feelings they think they can safely display. In stair-step progression, children learn which feelings to reveal based on the condition that the *previous* message was correctly understood *and* accepted by the parents. When parents fail to accept or understand one message, the child typically halts communication.

Notice in the following story that the father was first of all sensitive to his daughter's unspoken feelings. By continuing to "read between the lines" he was able to draw out what she needed to say. Also notice that by talking through her problem she was able to clarify her own thinking.

At dinner Jeane's father saw she was preoccupied and scarcely aware of the food she picked at. He knew it was not a time for their usual dinner-table banter. At the end of the meal he put his hand over hers and said, "Would you care to keep your old dad company in the family room for a while?"

They sat quietly on the couch for a few minutes; then Dad looked expectantly at Jeane, and asked softly, "Something at school today?"

Jeane sighed and nodded. "Lou Ann got in trouble for breaking one of Mrs. Riddell's plant vases." Her father recognized the emotion on her face. It was obvious to him that Jeane was concerned about more than her friend's misfortune.

"The punishment Lou Ann received made a strong impression on you." Dad waited for his daughter to continue.

"I know Lou Ann shouldn't have been clowning around where Mrs. Riddell keeps the plant vases. She got carried away and accidentally broke it. She was embarrassed to get yelled at. Then she had to miss the all-school movie. That kind of thing never happens to her." Dad looked on sympathetically and waited for Jeane to continue. She sighed again. "I probably should have gotten punished, too."

"Oh? Lou Ann wasn't the only one involved." There was interest in Dad's voice, but no condemnation.

"Mm-hm. I had been teasing Lou Ann, and she was teasing me back. It's just that she was noticed by Mrs. Riddell when the vase broke. I should have gotten in just as much trouble, because I was at fault, too."

"Even though you felt guilty about the whole incident, you didn't speak up. You were afraid you might be embarrassed by the punishment you could have received."

"Yeah. Daddy, I think I feel worse about it than Lou Ann."

"Feeling guilty was a form of punishment for you."

"Yeah. I need to talk to Mrs. Riddell about what we discussed. I'd feel better if she knew the whole story. Thanks for your advice, Dad."

Actually, Dad had given no advice. He had taken the role of an active listener and thus helped Jeane feel free to express a complete line of thought and emotion. She made a decision independently because she had been allowed to flow from one thought to another.

Imagine what would have occurred if Dad's very first response to Jeane had been drastically different. Jeane's initial statement revealed that her friend had been disciplined at school for misbehavior. An uninvolved father could have responded, "I would have spanked her if I had been the teacher," or "Lou Ann had it coming to her. That girl could stand a lesson or two in good behavior," or "I'd better not hear of you ever doing anything foolish like that."

Obviously, any such statement would not have encouraged Jeane to continue her line of thought in a fruitful manner. Rather, she may have chosen to lash out at her father in defense of her friend, or rudely told him what she thought of his callous attitudes, or left his presence knowing that her time was being wasted. However, instead of dismissing the incident with a single statement, her father allowed and encouraged Jeane to move step by step toward her own conclusion by making nonjudgmental responses.

One of the most common problems in communicating effectively with children is the parents' own discomfort in dealing with feelings. Our society teaches and encourages children and adults to hide their true emotions. We try not to allow others to know our real selves.

The irony of encouraging the withholding of emotion is that human nature works in the opposite direction. Emotions do not disappear just because they are not spoken. Earlier, we saw in the story of Randle that his suppressed expression resulted in his regularly soiling his pants. Children who fail to express their feelings can cause damage to others through inappropriate behavior, and as the following example shows, can harm themselves physically through the buildup of tension and stress.

Twelve-year-old Mitchell seemed to have everything going for him. He was known as one of the smartest boys in his class, and his teachers could depend on him to carry out his responsibilities. His family was considered "blue ribbon" and "all-American." His dad had the largest accounting firm in town. Mom, also, had a college degree and held a responsible position in a local business. Even though both parents were busy, they made an effort to spend time with Mitchell and his two older brothers. All three of their sons had been pleasant children, but there was something special about Mitchell: everyone seemed to like him the most.

Mitchell had complained of stomach problems occasionally as a younger child, but his reports of stomach pains had become more common during the last six months. Finally, his mother and father arranged for him to visit their family physician. After a thorough examination and several medical tests, the doctor determined the cause of Mitchell's complaints—a peptic ulcer.

Mitchell's family was surprised at the findings of the medical examination. They thought that only busy executives who rushed about under great stress got ulcers, not their twelve-year-old pride and joy! The physician referred Mitchell to my office for further psychological evaluation, which uncovered several important facts about this young adolescent.

An examination of Mitchell's weekly routine found him to be involved in a vast range of activities in addition to his regular school work. He was a member of both the school soccer team and tennis team. He was a Boy Scout who had achieved a large number of awards based on merit and accomplishments. Much to his dad's delight, he had expressed an interest in golf and was taking lessons from a local golf pro. He was active in church as a member of a children's choir and also of a hand bell ensemble.

In talking with me, Mitchell readily admitted that he was weary from being on the go all the time. He enjoyed some of his activities more than others, but felt obligated to continue all of them. He did not want to disappoint his parents, older brothers, friends, or instructors.

Several important emotions had been building in Mitchell for many of his twelve years without being expressed. These emotions included the fear of disappointing himself and others. Mitchell knew he needed to discontinue some of his activities, but simply did not know how to express his need for relaxation and a slower lifestyle. As a result, he was mentally and physically exhausted.

Mitchell's failure to communicate these needs to his parents did not cause his feelings to disappear, however. Rather, they were stored away in the form of tension and perfectionism. His mom and dad were given instructions to eliminate some of his outside activities. They also made an effort to be aware of Mitchell's feelings and presented him opportunities to express himself verbally, so that his body would not take the brunt of his emotions.

In addition to holding feelings within in the form of tension, children may express their feelings outwardly through misbehavior that can spell trouble for others who are in regular contact with them. Children who act out their emotions through misbehavior often sense that something is wrong, but are unable to identify and control the emotions that have a grasp on them. They continue patterns of behavior they recognize as self-defeating but are helpless to stop.

Tamara was a delightful fourteen-year-old girl in many ways. She was attractive and well thought of by her many friends because of her good nature. She made good grades in school and was looked on by her teachers as a student who had the potential to make something of herself. Tamara wore a smile on her face much of the time and could easily hold a conversation with adults.

Most of Tamara's friends were surprised by the rather sudden change in her behavior. Although her school grades remained relatively high, everyone knew she was not doing her best. She complained of the work that was assigned to her and was caught muttering obscenities at her teachers on several occasions.

Tamara's social behavior developed a more negative flavor as well. She became sassy among her friends and was quick to criticize those who she thought had acted wrongly. Many of her friends were stunned to learn that she had begun to associate with other students who had poor reputations. Stories circulated about her regular weekend abuse of alcohol. When Tamara's mother was convinced that her daughter's personal problems were creating too many disruptive behaviors, she sought help.

A story was pieced together over the course of two or three counseling sessions that explained Tamara's misbehavior. Her mother and father had divorced when Tamara was five years old. Her natural father made fairly regular contact with her, but was never committed to the psychological well-being of his daughter—and she was well aware of that fact! Mother had remarried to a man who was somewhat older and had never experienced fatherhood. Tamara was fond enough of him, but did not feel a special closeness.

Although Mother was aware that her daughter did not have a close relationship with a father figure, she did not know the depth of the void in Tamara's life. Through counseling she learned to listen to her daughter and encourage her to discuss some of her feelings. During one of their conversations, Tamara blurted out, "Well, you have Michael, but who do I have? Nobody!"

"You don't have Michael and me?" Mother asked gently.

"Michael is all right for a stepfather, but it's not like having my own father to take care of me," Tamara replied.

Mother had listened to the hurt. "I can see that your feelings about not having your own father run deep. I get the feeling your resentment over that has been building up inside you for a long time."

Tamara continued, "At first—after the divorce—I kept hoping that you and Daddy would get back together. I finally realized my wish would never come true. I couldn't tell you I was angry, because I could see that you were happily married to Michael."

"I can imagine the anger and loneliness you must have felt when I married Michael. It was a way for me to start my life all over, but you didn't feel the same way about him. I wonder how much of your resentment was directed toward me."

"Mom, I'm honestly glad that you've remarried and are happy with Michael. I'll admit, though, that sometimes when I mess around I hope that somehow you'll hurt inside the way I hurt."

Mother continued, "You've wanted very badly to be understood. I guess a lot of your misbehavior has been your way of crying out for help."

Tamara nodded. "A dumb way of telling you. Mom, do you think I can get turned around?"

Mother assured her that they would work on it, that she was on Tamara's side and was doing her best to understand. They ended that conversation with an embrace, and it paved the way for many more fruitful conversations. Tamara's acting-out behavior decreased over the next several weeks, her mood became more positive, and her friends and teachers remarked that she was her old self again.

Tamara had been aware that she was emotionally uncomfortable, but it was not until she and her mother began to talk freely and honestly that she was able to correctly identify the bitterness, jealousy, resentment, abandonment, and grief that were at the root of so much of her misconduct. Open communication allows children to come to conclusions about themselves. Through it they are not forced to accept what others say about their personal feelings, but choose their own words to correctly describe their characteristics.

By being willing to enter into open, honest dialogue, Tamara's mother displayed her belief that children are capable of making positive decisions on their own accord when given the opportunity. She allowed Tamara to express a complete train of thought—to express her emotional pain, recognize the negative impact she had on herself and others, and reach the conclusion that her misbehavior was a poor method of expressing her unhappiness. She had caused undeserved pain to others whom she loved.

Perhaps the most important message conveyed to a child who has been listened to in depth is one of love and affection. That child feels important and as valued as the most revered adult. Belonging to someone brings inner peace. And, as Tamara's story shows, that child can then focus on more positive forms of behavior.

*Teach them [God's commands] to*
*your children, talking about them*
*when you sit at home and when*
*you walk along the road, when you*
*lie down and when you get up*
(DEUT. 11:19 NIV).

# 26

# Creating a Special Time
# with Your Child

Mr. and Mrs. Becker sat in their living room one evening after their two children had gone to bed. Mrs. Becker had had an especially trying day with their eight-year-old son, Tony. She told her husband that, from the moment Tony walked into the house from school, she and the boy had been at odds with one another. "When I look back on the time I spent with Tony today, it seems that everything I said to him was negative. I hate to admit it, but I really did not enjoy being with him."

The problem Mrs. Becker described is not unique to her family. Many parents are not satisfied with the general quality of the interactions between themselves and their children. It seems they spend too much time being governor or housekeeper of their children, rather than as enjoyable and respected companions.

Children can become discouraged over a lack of quality time with their parents and may resort to various forms of misbehavior to communicate to their parents that they need encouragement and attention. Some misbehavior is quite obvious in nature, such as fighting with siblings, arguing with family members, or being obstinate and difficult to please. Other misbehaviors, more silent in nature, may include such acts as forgetting to complete assigned chores, giving half-hearted efforts, or moping about the house.

The natural tendency of most parents is to focus on the misbehavior of their children and to deal with it through discipline, rather than to understand the underlying causes of the misbehavior and attempt to eliminate them. One technique that has proven to be very helpful to parents of discouraged children is to establish a meaningful period of time during which the parent and child are in contact with one another. Below are ten steps toward establishing such a program.

1. Plan at least a fifteen-to-twenty-minute period each day to spend with your child. This can be a time your child normally plays alone, or it may be a special time you set aside. The time of day is unimportant. What is important is that it be a daily, uninterrupted period for you to be together.

2. Allow your child to select what he or she wishes to play or talk about. Give no help in this decision. This point is essential. By giving your child complete freedom in deciding on the type of activity, you communicate your interest in and respect for your child's interests.

3. Be relaxed in your approach to your child during this time. If your child wishes to play on the floor, it is important that you get on the floor, too, or if it is the wish, lie on the bed and talk. Always show you are willing to enter your child's world.

4. Ask no questions and give no commands during this special time. Because parents tend to communicate with children through questions and commands, this task may be difficult, but it will

avoid confrontations and make your child more relaxed and communicative.

5. Initially, note your child's activity for several minutes to formulate an idea of what he or she is doing and thinking. Stepping into your child's shoes, so to speak, and looking at the world through his or her eyes helps you to understand your child on a deeper level and communicate your understanding.

6. Occasionally describe what you perceive your child is doing and thinking at that time. In this way, you show your child that you are listening and noticing the things he or she is doing and thinking. This experience with parents is quite refreshing and even unburdening for a child.

7. From time to time, make statements to your child that provide encouragement. Responses that help your child evaluate his or her own activities are more helpful than responses that simply contain praise. For example, you may say, "You really worked hard to solve that puzzle," or "I certainly do enjoy listening to you talk about your activities at school."

8. Avoid correcting or disciplining your child during this time. If your child begins to misbehave, formulate a rule or guideline you will follow during your session. For example, state that the couch is not for standing on and that if your child chooses to continue doing so, you will choose to leave the play area until he or she behaves appropriately. It is important not to become involved in power struggles during this special time.

9. If other siblings ask to participate in your special time with your child, explain to them that this time has been set aside for you and the given child, and a period of time will also be set aside for them

later. Occasionally it is beneficial for a parent to play with all of the children in a group situation.

10. Realize that the technique of effectively attending to a child during a play period is not as easily done as said. At first you may feel somewhat awkward interacting with your child this way, but in time you will improve and feel more at ease. The effects of this type of attention are very positive. Parents are often amazed to see how responsive a child can be to their attention, even after years of negative interaction within the home.

During one of the conferences in which Mr. and Mrs. Becker and I discussed the communication gap between themselves and their son Tony, I gave them specific instructions for creating a special time with him. Both parents were willing to try anything to improve relations with him. Each parent agreed to create three special times with him over the next week. We would meet at the end of that week to discuss the effects of their efforts.

Both parents were surprised at the difficulty they had allowing Tony to express himself freely. Mrs. Becker said, "I had my first special session with Tony after school one day. Once he had put away his school things, I told him I had thirty minutes to do as he pleased. You would have thought that I had promised to give him the world for his birthday present.

"I have to admit that it was difficult for me to let him choose what we would play, but I did. I think he expected me to suggest a change in play activities, but I told him that he would be the one to decide how we spent our time. The hardest part was not telling Tony what to do while we played. I wanted too badly to make his decisions for him."

Mr. Becker added, "When I got home that evening after Tony and his mom had had their special time together, he couldn't wait to tell me what they had done. I think he felt relief that he and his mother had not spent the afternoon at odds with one another. It made a difference in the atmosphere in our home that evening. We were all more relaxed."

Mrs. Becker continued, "During one of my special times with Tony, he told me that sometimes he feels left out and all alone. I was rather shaken to hear my son talk that way. But I realized that he trusted me enough to tell me that. I said it must hurt to feel lonely and that no one cares about him. He seemed surprised that I understood, and was eager to tell me more. We spent most of that play time talking about some serious personal matters that were on his mind. I actually felt that I helped my son understand himself a little better, even though I never told him what my thoughts were on the topic."

Mr. and Mrs. Becker continued their "appointments" with Tony. They found that life with their son need not be burdensome, and recognized the benefits of entering his world and seeing life from his point of view. They learned that Tony was capable of making decisions without their constant input or supervision.

Above all, Tony began to feel he was more important in the eyes of his parents because of the time spent with each one without distractions. He no longer had to resort to misbehavior to get attention. His self-esteem improved, for he felt his function within the family was important and his opinion counted. His attitudes and behavior had changed for the better.

Children who do not have the opportunity to freely express themselves to those who are closest to them—their parents—feel doubt about themselves, and their psychological growth is stunted. But with a willingness to invest some time and energy, parents can be the most effective counselors their children will ever have. Then, children who have relaxed and positive attitudes about themselves will be free to develop concern for the parents who are close to them and for the people in the world beyond their families.

*I have found it of enormous value*
*when I can permit myself to*
*understand another person.*
CARL ROGERS

# 27

# Caught in the Buffer Zone

We have seen in chapter 9 that disunity between parents regarding the management of their children's behavior fosters an atmosphere where children tend to deceitfully manipulate their parents for their own purposes, which can further result in a general lack of respect for all family members. We also gave suggestions to help parents create a more harmonious atmosphere in the home.

In this chapter we shall examine disagreement between parents as being a communication problem and further probe its adverse effects on a child's self-concept.

Mr. and Mrs. Masters had invited some friends to their house one Friday evening for an informal visit, with coffee and dessert. Fifteen-year-old Shanda had no plans to be away from home that particular Friday night, but she did not relish the thought of spending the evening alone with her younger brother while Mom and Dad enjoyed themselves. She decided to resolve her dilemma by inviting a close friend to spend the night with her. She approached her father with the idea.

"Daddy, since you and Mom are having the Phillips here Friday night, would you mind if I invited Amy to spend the night at our house with me? I don't want to have to spend the whole evening with Shane; that would be too boring."

Dad briefly thought about his daughter's proposal before responding. "Your mom may not want to have Amy here the night we have company. I really don't see that it would do any harm, as long as you two girls don't make a lot of noise that would bother us. You probably should check with Mom, though, before you invite Amy."

With those encouraging words, Shanda began to make mental arrangements for her Friday evening activities. Perhaps she and Amy could style one another's hair, she thought, or read her latest teen fashion magazine, and listen to music on the stereo. They might even take turns calling boys on the telephone. Her excitement was already beginning to build! In the midst of her thoughts, she remembered that Dad had suggested she clear her plans with her mother. Shanda hurried into the den where Mom was.

"Mom, I asked Dad if Amy could spend the night with me Friday, and he said it would be fine! I'm going to call her to see if it's all right for her to come. I'm sure it will be. Her parents will let her!"

Mom stopped Shanda quickly. "Wait just a minute. I don't think Dad remembers that the Phillips are coming over for coffee and dessert. I don't think you should have Amy spend the same night we are planning to have company."

"But Mom! Dad *said* it would be all right as long as we stay out of your way. I promise we will. Besides, I don't want to have to spend my Friday night cooped up in this house with Shane."

"Shanda, your dad has no idea what kind of trouble he's creating. He's not the one who's planning the week-end, anyway; I am. He's constantly letting you kids do things he knows are going to make me mad! If he would use his brain half the time, he'd realize that all of us can't have company on the same night. Sometimes I wonder if he doesn't do these things just to give me a headache!"

As Mom and Shanda continued their argument, Dad walked into the room. He had heard his wife shouting and was angered at the accusations she had made of him. "Just a minute," he interrupted. "I don't see any reason Shanda can't have her friend over to this house the same night the Phillips are here. They'll stay in a different part of the house from us."

"Yeah," chimed in Shanda. "We won't bother you."

"And furthermore," continued Dad, "I told Shanda to ask you before she made definite plans for the weekend. I *do* use my brain most of the time!"

With that invitation to defend her statement about Dad's tendency to bungle family matters, Mom continued her verbal assault on her husband. And he reciprocated. Shanda watched quietly while her mother and father argued. Neither adult held back any words or negative feelings. Shanda felt she was caught in the middle of the battle between her parents and was somehow to blame.

Obviously, Shanda had used her father's encouragement as an opportunity to manipulate her mother into agreeing to her own plans. She certainly had been dishonest with her mother by stating that Dad had already unconditionally approved the plan.

The initial argument between Mom and Dad was over Shanda's being allowed to entertain her friend the same evening they had planned for their own visitors. It moved quickly, however, into a confrontation of wills between parents and away from that disagreement. How did it affect Shanda?

Shanda was angered because her parents' disagreement foiled her plans. Beyond her anger and disappointment, however, Shanda experienced guilt and shame over the lack of communication within her family. Even though she had a part in starting the argument by being less than honest with her mother, she assumed the burden of guilt over the whole battle between Mom and Dad, which went far afield from the original problem. This was not an isolated incident, however. Shanda had capitalized on an existing attitude between her parents to manipulate them. But the accusations and arguments between her parents were frequent, and Shanda always felt she was to blame.

While there are times a child should indeed have a genuine sense of guilt, guilt that is misplaced can be destructive. In Shanda's case, her guilt was a result of her incorrect assumption that it was she who was at fault for the continuing mistrust between her parents.

Children and adolescents are typically unable to fully realize who is responsible for troubles that befall a family. Because they assume that the world revolves around their thoughts and behaviors, the responsibility for bad communications between adults is frequently mistakenly placed on the wrong shoulders. Indeed, the load of guilt and shame often follows the adolescent into adulthood, causing unnecessary anxiety.

Carey was a college-aged female who came to my office for counseling. She had a long history of pent-up guilt and shame, and she could not remember a time when she was happy and content with herself. She recalled that during her childhood she felt strangely responsible for the severe conflict between her mother and father over petty matters of family business.

From Carey's point of view, too many of these parental disagreements had to do with her. In her naive way of thinking, her parents would have been far happier if she were not in their way. When she was age eleven and they divorced, she felt overwhelmingly responsible.

As an adolescent, Carey made two desperate suicide

attempts. She admitted that they were actually attempts to elicit joint attention and support from her mother and father—which they did not. She continued to feel that she was a failure, that her life did not count.

After a number of counseling sessions, Carey began to recognize the source of her sense of low self-worth. With effort she started to shed her incorrect assumptions about herself and for the first time in her life was able to see herself as a person of value.

Poor communication between parents can propel children down circuitous routes to guilt. Many children and adolescents gain great enjoyment from the sense of control they obtain when they create disagreements between their parents. Momentarily they may have the power to dictate when their parents will feel pleasant and when they will be angry and at odds with each other. The thrill of power often diminishes into feelings of shame, however, when children contemplate the results of their behavior.

Six-year-old Henry was a puzzle to his parents. They had tried everything within their power to teach him to comply with their requests. Yet, despite their best efforts, he continued to be difficult to control. Mom and Dad felt that in some way Henry was successfully manipulating them to give in to his demands for attention. Even though they loved Henry dearly, it was evident that he did not love himself. He would swing wildly from inappropriate showing off in social situations or blatant disobedience to either mopey withdrawal or whining and clinging to his parents.

As the communication patterns within this family were explored, it became evident that weaknesses existed that Henry recognized and exploited. Mom was stricter than Dad in most cases. For example, she would tell Henry to make his bed, only to discover later that Dad had helped him complete the task because "a six-year-old boy is too little to make his bed the right way."

Henry was well aware of these differences in his parents' childrearing practices. He leaned on his father to pull him from under many of the heavy demands placed on him by his mother. The payoff Henry received through Dad's unwillingness to allow him to be responsible for his own behavior was too great to turn down. He enjoyed having Dad act as a buffer for Mom's demands. But then, she constantly nagged at Dad for being too quick to meet the demands of their son.

On the one hand, Henry was being told by his dad, "I will take responsibility for the problems you must face." On the other hand, Henry perceived his mother to be saying, "My frustration with your father is a result of your behavior." He was putting himself in a predicament by taking advantage of his father, for he got the notion it was he who caused conflict between his parents. His quandry of craving attention and placing blame on himself worsened, and his guilt-induced behavior followed.

Children need clear communication among family members, but too often they become entrapped by the lack of it. It is frightening to realize that numerous youngsters can develop deep-seated guilt as a result of incorrectly interpreting the communication patterns of their families, guilt which they either act out or cover by actions that are harmful to themselves or others. Children at all ages need to feel valuable and to receive the kind of information about themselves from their families that give them good self-concepts. Much of that information is derived from messages between parents. Unity, and ideally, harmony between parents in turn ensures consistency in the communication from parents to children.

*Not by might nor by power,*
*but by my Spirit . . .*
(Zech. 4:6 NIV).

# 28

# Butting Heads

A mother raised her hand to ask a question following a talk I had given about family relationships. She stated that she and her ten-year-old daughter got along well most of the time. However, occasionally the two of them got into bad arguments, most of which centered around the mother's disapproval of her daughter's behavior. The mother admitted embarrassment over the intensity of these confrontations and requested guidance on how to handle such situations.

Confrontation. Should it be avoided at all cost? Is it inherently bad? Or is there such a thing as necessary and effective confrontation?

Most parents do not enjoy relationships with their children that are marked by constant butting of heads. True, some children and adults get an odd sort of enjoyment from a good argument, from winning a fight, from putting children or adults in their places. But even they get weary of such struggles and frequently end with guilt or defeatism or being terribly unsettled.

However, there are times when it is necessary to confront children to point out to them the error of their ways and at least begin to guide them along new ways. Such useful confrontation requires forethought as to purpose and procedure, which distinguishes it from a spontaneous and emotional reaction.

Baker was a ten-year-old boy who had a sharp tongue. He could exchange verbal jabs with the best of them. At times he used this "skill" as a way of having fun with others. At other times he put others in their place with a string of choice words. His parents, Mr. and Mrs. Hall, were concerned that Baker was unaware of the reputation he had built for himself through his way of talking to others. They felt he would alienate himself from his peers and eventually create more trouble for himself than he could handle. They had been told by some friends of theirs that one of the kindest things they could do for their son would be to point out this fault to him and help him see the negative way others perceived him.

Baker and his family attended a function at his school one Friday evening. Just as they walked up to the building, Baker spotted one of his classmates. "Hey Donald!" he yelled. "Way to flunk that math test in class today!" Donald ignored the statement while Baker chuckled out loud. His parents were embarrassed.

A few minutes later they saw their son approach the school's principal. Baker spoke loudly to her. "Hey, Mrs. Duke, did you get a stomachache after eating two desserts at lunch?" Mr. and Mrs. Hall cringed. They hoped they had not heard their son say *that* to his principal— surely not. But as they saw a scowl come over Mrs. Duke's face, they realized their ears had not played tricks on them.

As the night progressed, Baker made numerous rude remarks to other children and adults. His mom and dad were shocked at his behavior and intended to put a stop to it. After they got home, Baker was called into his parents' bedroom for a conference.

Dad began. "Baker, I was highly embarrassed at your

behavior tonight! There could *not* have been a parent at that school who was more ashamed of his son than I was of you. It was disgusting the way you talked to your friends, their parents, and even Mrs. Duke. I want an explanation for your behavior—and it had better be good!"

Baker took his father's statements in stride. "Aw Dad, I didn't mean anything when I said those things. I was just teasing. They all knew it."

"Teasing? You call that teasing? You might as well have carried a club with you to knock people on the head! None of those people looked to me as if they enjoyed your rude mouth. What do you have to say for yourself, young man?"

"Dad, just get off my back! I don't have to stand here and take this off you." With that, Baker turned to leave his father's room. Before he could, however, his dad caught him. More words were exchanged. The conversation ended with a sound spanking for Baker and a headache for Mr. Hall. Neither had come out of this confrontation in good shape.

Although Mr. Hall was correct in seeing the need to confront his son and do it in an appropriate setting (not make a scene at the scene) while the incident was still fresh, he used it as a means for venting his own frustration and turned it into verbal aggression.

There are several elements to keep in mind that can make confrontations effective. Paramount are understanding children's motives for their undesirable behavior, and maintaining visible respect for them. Children who feel misunderstood will disregard their parents' criticisms, and if they are disrespected as persons, will see no need to change.

Baker made his rude remarks as a way of being admired by his peers. Granted, his method was wrong, but his intentions were understandable. All children have a basic need to have a niche in their peer groups. Baker may also have been seeking approval from his family. Perhaps he thought his parents would be favorably impressed with him if they saw him as a comedian. Or, his rude behavior could have signaled a lack of social skills training.

If Mr. Hall had thought about this, he could have prefaced the confrontation by saying, "Baker, I realize you enjoy being noticed by your friends and teachers at school" or "It's tempting to say funny things to your friends so Mom and I can hear them." Baker could have, at that point, prepared himself for the criticism that was to follow, with the knowledge that his parents understood some of the reasons behind his behavior.

As has been emphasized throughout this book, solving children's problems is better accomplished when parents can view life from the child's point of view. It is not necessary for parents to *agree* with the logic of their child but to do their best to understand it.

Respect for the child is a necessary component of confrontation, since the display of respect from adult to child invites a similar response from child to adult. Mr. Hall felt much internal discomfort at Baker's rude public behavior. He showed disrespect for his son through the use of sarcasm. When Baker explained that his catty remarks were teasing, Mr. Hall told him, "You might as well have carried a club with you to knock people on the head!"

Baker quickly realized his dad's lack of respect and became defensive and unwilling to hear his words of criticism. He felt his worth as an individual had been denied and knew his dad was preparing to impose his own beliefs onto him. The opportunity for communication had vanished!

It is difficult to avoid judgment when it is necessary to confront children. Being older and wiser, parents know when their children have made mistakes as obvious as talking sassy to their friends and school principal. Yet, the children may not have reached that conclusion.

Respect for children allows them to develop insights about their behavior on their own. The confrontation is designed to help them along the way.

On hearing Baker's comments at school, his dad correctly concluded that his son needed to be made aware of the effect his remarks had on others. A helpful confrontation could have been, "Baker, tonight at school you made several comments that concerned me. I know you were excited to see your friends and you were glad Mom and I were with you. It's fun to be noticed by others. But, I feel that the way you got attention by saying unkind things defeated your purpose. I noticed that Donald hung his head, and Mrs. Duke wore a scowl on her face when you talked to them. Others will not want to be around you if you regularly talk to them as you did tonight."

Such a statement would let Baker know his father understood the reasons behind his behavior and respected him as a person of value and dignity. The focus would be entirely on the behavior and concern over its results for Baker and the others, rather than on his bad character or personality. In this manner, Baker could see that his father was correct in saying that it is fun to be noticed by others. He would be able to realize that his intentions (having fun with friends) and the potential outcome (having no friends with whom to have fun) did not match. He could then more readily accept the criticism of his behavior.

An additional payoff of an appropriate confrontation is that responsibility for a change in behavior remains in its proper position—with the child. In his confrontation with Baker, Dad assumed responsibility for seeing to it that his son changed his ways. Baker quickly saw that his father was upset and had a strong desire to avoid further embarrassment. Dad also implied that Baker was unreliable and likely to continue his disgusting behavior. Baker's reasons for wanting to leave his father's presence were clear: his father had the problem, and Baker had no desire to help him solve that problem.

The other suggested confrontational statement, however, is free of the emotional overtones of Dad's judgment and frustration. It assures Baker that his father will guide him, but he will not take the problem away from Baker and on himself. Baker continues to be the one who must learn to control his tongue.

Quite often when we confront children we want and expect an immediate change in behavior. But it is much more realistic to expect that an observable change in behavior will not come until some point in the future. Children need time to assimilate and act on the information they receive in a confrontation. Many times they will reject what they at first hear, only to find through the course of experience that their parents were right.

Remember, the purpose of confrontation is not to ventilate the parents' feelings, push children in desired directions, or pass judgment. The purpose of confrontation as an effective tool is to point out to children things of which they may have been unaware, in an effort to encourage them to responsibly change for their own and others' good.

*He who is forgiven little, loves little*
(LUKE 7:47 RSV).

# 29

# Erasing Mistakes

Can you imagine a world without mistakes? If no people made mistakes, there would be no disagreements, no accidents, no unkindness. A mistake-free world would have no war, no poverty, no destruction. Human life would not know such things as divorce, child abuse, alcoholism, racism, and crime. Can you imagine such a world? Neither can I.

We live in a world marked by one mistake after another. The disharmonies between individuals, families, organized groups, and nations are all direct results of series of mistakes.

Thus, a reality of life is that we must face mistakes— our own and those of others. The way we deal with the mistakes of family members has a tremendous impact on the overall communication among family members. Few parents are so naive or so proud that they refuse to admit their children make mistakes or that they themselves are prone to error. Yet, failure to accept the fact that a mistake has been made by the child or parent severely hampers family relationships.

Stephen came to my office a troubled sixteen-year-old boy. He was bitter toward his father, for he could do nothing to please the man. Everything he did brought criticism and shame from his dad. As a result, Stephen had an unhealthy opinion of himself and slipped away into self-destructive behavior. He began to consume alcohol regularly and became intoxicated almost weekly. His parents were aware of and rather embarrassed by his promiscuousness with girls. He had been caught stealing items from his own house and from his friends. Stephen was well on his way toward juvenile delinquency.

Stephen told me about his relationship with his father and the way he fell constantly under the man's scrutiny. Nothing positive he did seemed to be good enough for his father, but his father noticed and acted on everything negative.

Stephen told me, "My dad has said several times that he would put my past behind me and let me start all over again. But the next time I did something wrong, he would bring up my past mistakes and tell me how I've shamed him as a son. I've just done too many wrong things now for him to ever forgive me."

After gaining Stephen's trust, I suggested that he and I meet jointly with his father so he could share with his father the emotions he had shared with me. Stephen was both excited and afraid for our conference. After a tentative beginning, the adolescent began to bare his soul before his father. He described the hatred that had grown within him through the years. He told of how difficult it had become to see himself in a positive light. He explained that he knew that he had done wrong by involving himself in illicit behaviors. The experience was one of cleansing and release for Stephen.

Stephen was astonished at the reply he received from his father. He expected to receive another tongue lashing, or a lecture about how to straighten up and fly right. However, his dad did not react in this predictable, negative manner.

"You know, Stephen," began his dad in a low tone of voice, "you've told me all those things before, but I have never really listened to you. I've always felt that I should be tough on you so you wouldn't make more and more mistakes. But I see that my tactics have backfired. I never realized what a negative influence I've had on you. You need me to forgive and forget all that you've done, and *this* time that's really what I'll do. I hope you can do the same for me."

Stephen believed his father. He recognized the lack of condemnation in Dad's voice and in its place a sincerity that had been absent before. Time proved Stephen's belief to be correct. His father dealt with his mistakes separate from the past and emphasized helping Stephen rather than shaming him.

Stephen later confided, "Now that my dad is able to put my past behind me, it's easier to look at ways I can improve myself. It didn't used to bother me to make my dad angry, but now I'm trying harder to please him."

Forgiveness is a concept that is more difficult to grasp than is readily apparent, but I see it as a major ingredient in open communication. Forgiveness involves more than simply forgetting a past wrong. It entails the re-establishment of a broken relationship. It is not humanly possible to forget all the wrongs that have been delivered over a period of years. It is possible, however, to place the importance of a relationship above that of a mistaken behavior.

In the case of Stephen, we see the effects of the failure to forgive on the life of an adolescent boy. Although Stephen's father had told his son that his past was forgotten, it was not. Why was his father unable for so long to be forgiving? One of his primary concerns was the effects of his son's behavior on his own reputation. Admittedly, no parent would choose to be known as the mother or father of a bad kid. Because of the threat of this stigma, a parent may, as Stephen's father did, choose to be harsh and punitive as a way of preventing embarrassing behavior. Too often the parent searches for a punishment strong enough to deter acting out. As with Stephen, though, that tactic backfires in most cases, for it breaks the relationship even further.

We've already seen that children and adolescents who feel misunderstood will find some way of expressing themselves. Stephen could not communicate to his father his need for understanding; thus he chose to assert this need through negative behavior. It was not until his dad recognized Stephen's need for forgiveness and understanding to mend the relationship that he changed his focus from the effects of Stephen's behavior on his own reputation to the emotional needs of the boy.

A second reason for Dad's failure to forgive was Stephen's failure to live up to his expectations of him. Stephen's father had long hoped his son would have a successful academic career and join him in the family business. He placed tremendous stock in Stephen's accomplishments and had projected onto him his own hopes and dreams. When he thought he could not count on Stephen to fulfill those dreams, bitterness ensued. Yet, as the man relinquished his hold on the course of Stephen's future, he was able to derive more pleasure from his son's newly found responsibility and motivation toward life.

Stephen's experience with his father brings into clear view two communication needs of children. The first is that they need to know they can reveal anything to their parents without fear of condemnation. They must realize that, while disciplinary action may be the consequence of their behavior, forgiveness will never be withheld.

Second, children must be assured they will never be cut off from their families. Rejection does not bring about growth. In a healthy relationship, parents communicate to their children an understanding of their needs and a willingness to support them rather than hammer away at their personal flaws.

June and her mother were having a heated exchange.

Several days earlier June had been disciplined for participating in an incident in school. Her school principal was uncertain of June's involvement, but chose to punish her because circumstantial evidence suggested she was guilty. June's mother, Mrs. Kilgore, agreed with the principal's decision to punish her daughter, since she would learn a lesson whether or not she was guilty.

One of June's friends later confessed to being responsible for the misdeed and exonerated June from all wrongdoing. Her principal apologized to her and telephoned Mrs. Kilgore to inform her of her daughter's innocence. However, Mrs. Kilgore was not sympathetic toward her daughter.

"But Mom," June pleaded, "don't you see that I had nothing to do with what Sherry did? I was just standing there by her locker when she started drawing on it with her marker. I told her she shouldn't do it, but she didn't listen!"

"You shouldn't have been standing there in the first place! Sherry is constantly talking you into doing wrong. I've told you to stay away from that girl!"

"But Mom, don't you see? I wasn't doing anything wrong! Mr. Wilson told you that. He even apologized for punishing me. Why are you still so angry with me?"

"Mr. Wilson said you weren't guilty *this* time. That doesn't mean you won't be guilty the next time you and Sherry do something." Mom refused to budge from her position.

"Well, you're wrong, Mom! I didn't do anything wrong. Mr. Wilson even says so. Why won't you admit it?" With those words June burst into tears.

Communication between June and her mother ended because Mrs. Kilgore refused to admit to a mistake and held a grudge against her daughter despite evidence she had been innocent.

In addition to forgiving the child for a negative act, the parent must provide the child the opportunity to also exercise forgiveness. The words, "I was wrong" or "I am sorry" open the way for the child to pardon the parent.

Many parents feel uncomfortable asking forgiveness from their children. Mrs. Kilgore certainly fit into that category. Behind this woman's words and behaviors could have been the belief that the admission of being mistaken is equivalent to giving power or control to the child. Perhaps she believed it not in her child's best interest to show signs of weakness. Whatever her motivation, communication between her and her daughter was severely damaged.

Parents' willingness to admit mistakes facilitates communication in a number of ways. It makes them psychologically accessible. By knowing their parents are also error prone, children see them as more human. They feel less guilty for making mistakes because they have seen their mothers or fathers in similar situations.

The admission of wrongdoing by parents also serves to promote a feeling of safety and warmth within the home. In section 1 we discussed in detail the responsibility of parents to create an atmosphere right for psychological growth. Honest parents assure children that all family members are of equal worth who are in the process of growing, changing, and improving. Acknowledging and correcting errors is part of that process.

The parent who fails to admit wrongdoing provides a poor role model for the child. Mrs. Kilgore taught June a lesson during their exchange. Unfortunately, it was an unhealthy lesson. June learned that one way of dealing with shortcomings is through denial. Mrs. Kilgore was unwilling to admit her error. She failed to look at a problem objectively and to see the situation from her daughter's point of view. June observed this behavior—and learned from it.

To deal with daily errors honestly also creates the opportunity for responsible problem solving. The child is better able to face problems realistically and to be more open minded. Mrs. Kilgore tried to show June that her association with Sherry frequently resulted in trouble of one type or another. Yet June was unable to consider that problem because of her mother's inflexibility in admitting an error. If her mother had admitted her mistake, she could have then helped June to move on to the more basic issue of Sherry's influence on her. Instead, she closed the door to further communication.

In this chapter we have seen that the parent who can accept a child's shortcomings opens the way to forgiveness and a mended relationship. The parent who can admit to having been mistaken is indeed a strong person, but in the eyes of the child is more human and likely to be forgiven. In such an atmosphere healthy dialogue and problem solving can take place.

# Afterword

I had seen Mr. and Mrs. Richards in several counseling sessions. The focus of our session had been on their struggling relationship with their adolescent daughter. We had covered a wide range of issues about their family, many of which have been presented in this book.

With a simultaneous smile and sigh of mental exhaustion, Mrs. Richards said, "You know, it's hard to believe the complexity of the connection between the parent and child. I'm learning that I must approach my role as a parent with the knowledge that I'll never be an expert. But, I've learned how to step back from my role as a mother and view myself more objectively. That one skill has made a tremendous difference in my effectiveness with my daughter. I still don't always know if I'm doing or saying the right thing to her. I've learned, though, that I can't be a good parent by simply reacting to my own emotions. I know that in time I'll get better at my job."

Mrs. Richards was right. The connection between the parent and child is complex. Mrs. Richards will be increasingly effective as a parent because of her desire to learn of the intricacies of family relations.

I have viewed the parent-child relationship through three major areas of focus: the home atmosphere, behavior management techniques, and effective communication. Although it is a complex relationship and does require effort to master even very few of the skills to be successful, the parent-child relationship is one that can be most rewarding and satisfying.

I encourage you in your parenting efforts. May God bless you and those you love.